Sun Breaks Through Gray Skies:
The Dharma Lives in Cleveland

A Year of Dharma Talks by
Sensei Ji Sui Craig Horton
of the Cleveland Buddhist Temple

Compiled and Edited by:
Prof. Stefan J. Padfield

Cover Art by:
Tim Averre

The Cleveland Buddhist Temple

These talks were all recorded at the Cleveland Buddhist Temple, 1573 E 214th St., Cleveland, OH 44117. At the time of this writing, the Temple is experiencing serious financial difficulties threatening its ability to keep its doors open. Donations are greatly appreciated. The Temple's website can be found at www.clevelandbuddhisttemple.com.

Editor's Introduction

Sensei Horton told me it was delusional to write a book about Zen. I can think of no better introduction to testify to his wisdom. I am also reminded of a story Sensei Horton told about a monk who delivered the same dharma talk every day for a week. By the end of the week, there were far fewer students in the audience than at the beginning. After finishing his final rendition of the talk, the monk said: "Now you can make this story your own."

Finally, I doubt reading these talks will always be easy. There is a tension, I believe, between staying true to the spoken word and readability. I have purposefully chosen to err on the side of staying true to the spoken word. However, I believe that if you approach the reading with a meditative attitude, whatever effort you must expend will be rewarded. I hope you enjoy Sensei Horton's dharma talks as much as I have.

All rises and falls.
Suddenly, this consciousness.
I bow in Gassho.

"Rise" and "fall": empty.
Beyond this consciousness: One.
There is no bower.

Beyond emptiness,
Beyond even the Oneness,
Para Sam Gate.

Namaste,
Stefan J. Padfield, Editor

Editor's Acknowledgments

I would like to thank Shirley Nook for her kind editorial assistance.

I would also like to thank my wife, Dr. Maria Pagano, for listening.

Stefan J. Padfield

TABLE OF CONTENTS

1. Instructions
2. "The flowers do not bloom for you."
3. "Are you living in the dharma or in your beliefs?"
4. "What is wrong with the dharma?"
5. "Chickens have two legs, horses have four."
6. "Our life is unexplainable."
7. "When 'good' and 'bad' disappear, things can be as they are."
8. "While you are trying to become something, your true nature is arriving here and now."
9. "All arise from the same source."
10. "Your life is in your hands."
11. "Drink in the dharma."
12. "Sitting in ignorance."

13. "Are you enjoying your life?"

14. "Beware of your conclusions."

15. "Difficult is it to hear the teaching of the Blessed One."

16. "Things are not what they seem to be, nor are they otherwise."

17. "How are you?"

18. "Do not seek enlightenment."

19. "Just sit for twenty years."

20. "Just sit."

21. "Who will be kind to your life, if not you?"

22. "Beyond form, into the Sangha."

23. "Does the dharma need your 'happiness'?"

24. "Does the dog have Buddha nature? There is no dog."

25. "Who is sitting?"

26. "Show only one face to all things."

27. "Who are you to say that This is not 'The Way'?"

28. "What you are seeking is empty."

29. "You are an infinite possibility."

30. "When will This be enough?"

31. There is no 'more' in This."

32. "Lose yourself in this breath."

33. "There is actually nothing to do."

34. "Arriving in this breath—no suffering."

35. "There is nothing 'short' or 'long' about a life—there is just life itself."

36. "Why buy a cookbook when you are hungry? Just eat!"

37. "[A]ll thought is a 'future event.'"

38. "Drop it!"

39. "Holiday"

40. "Have a cup of tea."

Instructions[1]

> *There is no one to struggle with, just simply count your breath.*

There are sounds from the outside and thoughts from the inside. Let them come, then let them go. If they return, let them return. Then let them go with your next deep exhalation.

Do not be fooled by conceptual ideas such as "good" or "bad", "right" or "wrong", "happiness" or "unhappiness", "comfortable" or "uncomfortable". Have no preference. Just sit, and count your breath. Your thoughts are like passing clouds in a blue sky. Sit in the blue sky. Let them go. Ordinary mind is the way.

Sit like a mountain. The rain may fall, snow may come, the wind may blow, but a mountain just sits. Empty yourself

---

[1] Editor's Note: Sensei Horton freely acknowledges that he frequently borrows from the sayings of others in his dharma talks—only sometimes identifying the source. I have not attempted to track down every original source.

of everything and become a true mountain. Ordinary mind is the way.

Zazen is not practiced in time. To arrive in time is to suffer. Zazen is this breath, and beyond.

Do not be fooled by your thoughts. Return to counting your breath. Each breath is your life—inhalation, exhalation. Sit in your life.

To study the dharma is to study the self. To study the self is to forget the self. Wake up to others. When this is forgotten—true awakening.

Sitting quietly, doing nothing, spring comes and the grass grows by itself. Arrive nowhere else except here.

"The flowers do not bloom for you."

> *[P]eople are like flowers. They arrive. They have a karmic path. They are not here for your pleasure. . . . [A] lot of them are still in what we would call the mud, or the dirt, or the manure. You cannot see them as they will be when they bloom.*

Earlier today I was talking to a young man. Over the past few days he has been irritated by everyone he has encountered. Yes, irritated with everyone. So they ask: "What's wrong with him?" I said: "I'll ask him because I don't know."

So we talked and I said: There are flowers that bloom. These flowers that are blooming did not come here to make you happy. They have a karmic path. They have no name. They are not here to make you happy. These flowers arrive on their karmic path and they continue. They do not compare themselves with each other or anything else. They do not care whether they are a rose, a magnolia, a dandelion, or whatever. They do not even care about their color. They arrive and they are living in the dharma. And their lives are going forward. They are being themselves.

Other people are like flowers. They arrive. They have a karmic path. They are not here for your pleasure. And they go on.

So, here we are with these flowers that we wish to control, give them names, add morals to them, decide their value and everything else. Are they being hindered in this way, or are we assisting them in their karmic path—helping them just as they are? I told him that a lot of them are still in what we would call the mud, or the dirt, or the manure. You cannot see them as they will be when they bloom.

There is a teaching about a Zen master who plants a fig tree when he is eighty years old. And a young man walks up and says, "Old man, why are you planting that fig tree? You will not be here to see it bear fruit. You will not be here to see it." And the old man said, "There were fig trees here before me, and I wish for them to be here after me." So, these flowers that are blooming, and those in the manure and everything else, can we stop hindering them and let them go on their karmic path? You may not be here to see what that future is as it arrives or blooms in the here and now. But can we assist?

"Are you living in the dharma or in your beliefs?"

> *I live out of sync. I live in the belief of "better." I sit to become better. Instead of sitting in the dharma . . . .*

Here we are. Maybe a day ago, using linear time, it snowed. Conditions were just perfect and the snow fell. There was nothing we had to do to make it happen. It did not fall for us. Just like the flower. But we live in its experience—just like we live in the kindness of others. The kindness of the flowers. The kindness of the snow.

Yet and still, it does what it does. It is not saying, "I am going to try and be kind to you." It is its nature, the way it is. But me, I live out of sync. I live in the belief of "better." I sit to become better. Instead of sitting in the dharma, I sit in a belief that down the road I will get better. I compare this moment with another down the road or some future where I will be better. That comparison is simply like trying to compare the breath. This breath that I take right here cannot be compared with any other breath. The flower cannot be compared with any other flower. Absolutely right there. Absolutely this breath. The dharma. There is no "better." Arriving into this breath.

Now, I can arrive into the belief or delusion or suffering that if I sit, then somewhere in the future I will be better, kinder, more. Or, I can live in the dharma.

So one may ask, "How are you enjoying your life? How are you doing?" Are you living in the dharma or in your beliefs? Your life is very, very short.

So, here we are. Living a very, very short life. The dharma is like the flower, the candle, the incense, the snow that fell. It is the conditions. These conditions. Am I assisting or altering them? Assisting, I would say I am doing nothing. Non-action. Yes. Beyond the good and bad, the kindness and unkindness. I am the dharma. Natural. Just like the flower on its karmic path.

Sometimes I may sit and the mind may go blank. Nothing there except This—whatever it is—and beyond. Others may be writing or reading or watching something and the mind goes blank. Practicing zazen, arriving here in this breath. Or, the mind may go to: "I am frustrated." So, I will go to the breath. And stopping and pausing in it—it empties. And a natural-like state may appear.

So, where am I? Am I enjoying my life? Am I enjoying the dharma, which is my life? Or, am I enjoying my beliefs, which is suffering?

How many of you are sitting to get "better"? More peace. More serenity. As if there is such a thing, you are sitting to get "better".

One day I was sitting right here. It was either Hanamatsuri or Obon. Sensei Ogui came here and asked me, "Why are you sitting?" I had no answer, and he left. Why are you sitting? Is there an answer? Is there a "you"? In the Boddhisattva's vow[2] we speak of the flesh and blood, the incarnation of Buddha. Incarnation into this delusion and beyond. So, things are not what I think they are. People, as

---

[2] Please see Appendix I.

they enter into my life, they do not do what I want them to do. They have this karmic path. They're not what they seem to be. They are the incarnations of the Buddha. Clothes, protections of life, all kinds of stuff. But, they have strange names: Dave, John, Stefan, all kinds of stuff. And they seem to be separate from the truth or the dharma. They stand out. And they have "attachments" to them. I ask myself: Who made it this way? Who put these attachments on? "I'm supposed to do this, and this, and this." We seek "more." Study more. Find out more about the five skandhas or aggregates. Not realizing that these things are empty. Just Buddha. No "dog that has Buddha nature." No "Buddha nature." Just mu. No self.

So, do I arrive in the dharma or am I arriving in my beliefs that somewhere down the line life is going to be good—I will have more peace, things will go smoothly. Yes, I will disappear. I will follow the breath down into the belly and back up. I am going to do all these things. And even with this form, never really escaping from the one who is suffering.

The one who says, "I will." So, "I will take care of that"—whatever it is. I've been habituated to say that. It traps me here. I have not yet awakened. "I'll take care of that. Yes, we'll do that—someday." So, am I living in these beliefs or in the dharma?

"What is wrong with the dharma?"

> *We talk about philosophy, realization, interdependence, impermanence, the middle path, and a whole bunch of other things. But how do we implement these things in our life? Do we use the intellect that believes it is in the light, or believes it is looking for the light, or that it can obtain the light? Or do we rely on others?*

In a dharma talk, one may always say, "Thank you for your kindness." Also, one may say, "The reason your beliefs aren't here is because you showed up." That is why you cannot find your beliefs. You arrive in every breath, every flower that blooms, every snowflake that falls. So, this is your life, not your belief.

Buddhism talks about interdependence. Without you—that karmic path—none of the others could be here. So, your beliefs are your suffering and the delusion. Stay in the breath and stay at rest. Breathing in. Breathing out. Life itself. Beyond birth and death.

Earlier today I was talking about what either my mother or grandmother used to say. She said, "Boy, you couldn't get out of a paper bag even if you had a flashlight in the dark." She saw that I was lost in beliefs, delusions and everything else. I was a little kid. It was almost like I just could not follow directions. Also, I said that in another place there is a reading that says, "You did not find my light. Rather, I came crashing into your darkness." And the last thing that I said—all quotes from something else—"To experience the light you must remain in the dark."

All of these statements talk about a genuine humility and infinite wisdom and boundless compassion. In Taoism they have the Yin and Yang circle. One dark, one white. Little black, little white. And this is a circle of harmony. Both of these compliment each other. Some may even call it the middle path. Some may call it that which is beyond dichotomy—good and evil, right and wrong. What is beyond these things?

So, here we are. Something has shown up and here we are at the Cleveland Buddhist Temple. Sitting that doesn't make any sense, walking and chanting that doesn't make any sense. But yet and still, this is what we do. I'm even dressed funny and it doesn't make any sense. [*Laughter.*] Flowers are dying, candles and incense are burning away. Conditions are constantly changing. And I am here believing that I may obtain enlightenment, realization. Yes. I come here because I know these are the things that I am looking for. But yet and still, I am still not in the dharma. Knowing is light. Not knowing is the dark. How do we bring these together? How do we bring the five skandhas that we cannot completely extinguish together with infinite wisdom and boundless compassion?

Some of the things we talk about are things like the Eightfold Buddhist Path. We talk about philosophy, realization, interdependence, impermanence, the middle path, and a whole bunch of other things. But how do we implement these things in our life? Do we use the intellect that believes it is in the light, or believes it is looking for the light, or that it can obtain the light? Or do we rely on others? Everything has what they call "Buddha Nature"—it is the dharma. Do we rely on others? Do we use the phrase, "Namu Amida Butsu"—calling on wisdom and compassion from the other shore? What do we use?

So, here we are at the Cleveland Buddhist Temple. Now, who here is looking for enlightenment? Craig always used to look for enlightenment. That's what he would come here for. One would say, "For what reason do you need it? Do you want to impress your friends? For what reason do you need it?" Nature itself, before the mind distorts it, is already beyond enlightenment. Beyond that limited world. It is infinite, constantly changing. To use the word is to limit it to a construct that is in my mind. But it is beyond that.

So, sitting in the dharma the Buddha once said: "This is delusion." And it disappeared. His mind had been producing it and everything else. What did he see? Maya? The daughters? What did he see? He tried to transmit this message over his lifespan of 80 years. Sitting. And in some books they called it "sermons" as the words changed, as it became westernized. But he tried transmitting the dharma. And he did it in a rare form. Very rare. In koans. In riddles. In things that would stop the mind from thinking.

To receive the light, one must stay in the dark. Things aren't what they seem to be, nor are they otherwise.

The teacher asks, "What do you say?" Some come up with: "My heart is beating"; "I'm sitting right here"; or, "It's too soon to tell." They use words they have been trained by the mind to come up with. But once this training disappears, what words come up? Or do any words come up? Perhaps there is just a smile. You have already gone beyond such limited views.

How did the teacher know when Mahakassappa received the dharma via the twirling of a flower? What expression was on his face when that message was transmitted? It did not come in words.

So, what do you hear? Not the things that mind has gravitated to: "It's too soon to tell"; "I'm sitting right here"; or, "My heart is beating." These are things we were trained to say.

There's another story about a kid whose Zen master would walk around and wag his finger every time someone would say something. And so the kid was going around imitating the master. Every time someone would say something, the kid would wag his finger at them. Then one day the master caught him and said something to him and the kid wagged his finger and the master cut off his finger—and the kid was enlightened. He woke up. That's right. Very simple things. Waking a person up. What would that mean— to cut off the finger and become enlightened? Some people still read that story and try to figure it out. What does that mean? Chopped the finger off, then the kid ran away, then he looked at his finger, and then he became enlightened.

So, here we are, in the dark, sitting. We want enlightenment, awareness, a little peace. What are we looking

25

for? Is it in words? Maybe we are sitting in the dark waiting for the light to come. Light is going to be here soon. Let me see if I can get rid of this thought, come back to the breath. But what are we waiting for? And why is it needed? It's almost as if someone has told you a story of a mystical place that doesn't exist. You read this story and you believe that it is true. Wow, this is a great story. I wish I could go there. What is wrong with the dharma right here? The way things really are. But I wish I could go somewhere else, to this great other place. This place in my head where I'm going to become a Buddha.

You hear another story about a student sitting and the master asks him, "Why are you sitting?" And the student answers, "To become a Buddha." And the master takes a rock and he starts polishing it and says, "I'm going to make a mirror out of this." And the student was thus enlightened.

What are you sitting for? This is it.

So, here we are. Sitting in the dharma. And we are looking for something. My teacher said, "We are standing in water up to our necks and we are dying of thirst." Quit reading fairy tales. Thank you.

"Chickens have two legs, horses have four."

> *[W]hen you are sitting in the heat, just sit in the heat and sweat. Do not wish for things to change. Since the heat is there, sit with it and experience your life. . . . [T]hese extremes are impermanent.*

Earlier today, just before the sitting, a woman asked me what the dharma talk was going to be about. I told her I did not know what the dharma talk was going to be about. So, she was just about to give me a topic when I told her I'd suddenly realized what it was going to be. I'm going to talk about something that most of us struggle with. That is, not wanting things the way they are. Yes.

So, in the summertime we sit here and it is very, very hot. We wish that it was cooler. In the wintertime we sit and it is cold outside. And we wish that it was warmer. My teacher once said, "Craig, when you are sitting in the heat, just sit in the heat and sweat. Do not wish for things to change. Since the heat is there, sit with it and experience your life." He also said that these extremes are impermanent. So, have wisdom and compassion. Why are you wishing for things to be different? In connection with this he gave a koan that says, "Chicken have two legs, horses have four. Summer flowers are blooming more and more." Or in the wintertime he would say, "Snow is falling more and more." And, he stated that these things will be like this no matter what you want. So, why do you want anything to be different? Chickens have two legs, horses have four. The snow is falling more and more.

He would always ask, "Are you enjoying your life?" Did you wake up to this truth?

Another thing he said was that the words that we use while wishing that it was a little warmer or a little colder point to extremes. He talked about the middle path that leads to neither side, where both seem to just disappear so you are just there.

So, a while back the carpet here was a little different color. The cat had scratched a hole in it back there and the linoleum was white with concrete under it. The boiler downstairs worked when it got ready to. And it was very cold. You could see your breath sometimes. And people would come here with their scarves and coats on and we would sit. And the floor would be cold, so we wore a lot of socks. But we would sit. Not wishing for it to be warmer. But the cold seems to be like it says in the reading—the avatar of the Buddha. It helped us to move beyond, or emancipated us from this karmic path of delusion of wishing it was warmer…wishing that it was this or that. Seeing that we are here with the cold, so why not? Yes. Just sit.

People would ask him questions and he would grunt and tell them to go sit over there. "When are we going to get the boiler fixed?" Yes. Good question, isn't it? Makes sense. It is cold in here so when are we going to get the boiler fixed? He would just grunt and say, "Go sit down." You don't have to worry about it. These conditions are impermanent. You don't have to worry about when. So, for that time we sat in the cold. Then, one day we sat in the heat. The next time we sat in new quarters. New carpet. Just sit in This, not "When?"

The breath that we use going in and out has no preference. It has no preference. If it is cold, it sits and breathes there. It has no preference about the heat or when the boiler is going to be fixed. So, one would say you wake up to the fact that chickens have two legs, horses have four, and the snow is falling more and more. And one may smile at oneself when that thing arises in the head: "When is this thing going to happen?" Go back to counting your breath.

Thank you. That will be all of my dharma talk.

"Our life is unexplainable."

> *"Sitting" does not have to mean sitting on a cushion. "Zen meditation" does not mean I must be sitting still somewhere. It means a state of mind that says, "Yes. My mind is aware. Open."*

In the Zen practice of sitting, even after the practice there may be no words—just experience. So, one may not say anything. But the bow, and the facial expression, tells all. Here one may say, "I am honored to have sat with you." Or one may say, "Thank you for your kindness, which made such an event possible." Also, we live in the kindness of others, so others have assisted us—the seen and the unseen; the liked and the disliked. Going beyond any dichotomy and knowing about oneness—that all of these things have made my life possible.

I was talking, not too long ago, about the rain falling, the wind blowing, the cars making noise, and other things that were not seen that were there—and I never quite paid attention to them. But I paid attention to the fresh thought that came into my mind. Separating myself from the very things that make all this possible—the pictures around me; the incense; the candle.

Something strikes a person. Not in sitting, but while walking around they may have hit their foot, something may have dropped on their head, a bird may have done its little business, and all of a sudden they are awakened. They are awakened by conditions that were outside their awareness. Yes, we know how to sit, breathe, and everything else. That is practice. But other conditions make that possible.

A lady was here the other day and she put on her sweater when the wind blew through the door. I asked her whether it was her choice to put on her sweater or did she put it on because of the wind. So, the conditions awaken me to life itself. Free the mind of suffering and move with the conditions—conditions that arise of infinite wisdom and boundless compassion. I normally move by limited self. I have a plan—what I'm going to do. How I'm going to do it.

Where I'm going to be. What I have to do later on. What I'm going to become. And everything else. I have a plan.

But my teacher once said, "Things do not go the way you planned." Why not? Because the wind might hit a piece of your hair and you might have a thought and everything will change. So he said, "Why not be one with the conditions you have arrived in?" This breath arrives into these conditions. Free the mind, and just sit in these conditions. "Sitting" does not have to mean sitting on a cushion. "Zen meditation" does not mean I must be sitting still somewhere. It means a state of mind that says, "Yes. My mind is aware. Open. Free of dichotomy, entanglement, and everything else that is coming in." So, I try to be aware of my conditions.

Sometimes these things or possibilities happen to us on a mountain, in a park, at the lake, washing a dish, doing an exercise. Some runners call it a "high." Or, they may lose themselves and things seem effortless—becoming a part of the conditions. And in these states one might ask, "How far can this go?" Look around and all will be infinite possibility.

So, what was your possibility today? What truly happened to you? If you use memory, it will be limited—very limited—to the things you believe you have seen and how they came together. Very limited. You may have seen a couple of people, drove a couple of places, went to the job, did some work. Very, very limited. Your memory will not have the rain, the sun, the shine. It will not have the wind, the air. It will not have the little chips on the side of the road, the grass, the trees. It will not have the infinite possibilities. It will be limited to your understanding, and it will be "memorized." But the things that made it all happen will not be there. Only the things that you believe are important. The one million, two million, three million things that you may believe—that is all that will be there.

So, when we see from this limited view, our lives seem to just be made up of going to work, doing this and that, etc. But when we see the infinite possibilities, our life is unexplainable. Yes. We awaken into possibilities that could not be foreseen. It will no longer be this limited view of what we are creating, but rather this infinite possibility of what we are receiving. Yes, receiving. Sitting here and receiving.

So, one may say, "I put myself in the Buddha . . . in the dharma . . . in the sangha, because I am receiving from infinite possibilities." Someone will come up with a thought that will feel like it is an original idea. Some others will see things that have never existed until now. They will wake up there. But all our lives, in every breath, have never existed until now. Why are we asleep? It has never existed till now. Why are we asleep?

So, each breath I arrive into what never existed till now. I do not really find this amazing because I do not really do what Dogen or any of the other teachers say: To study the self; to forget the self; and to be others—one with others, with these infinite possibilities. Or in Jodo Shinshu, one with Amida Buddha, Sakyamuni Buddha—infinite possibilities. They pointed to something that sometimes they needed words to say. Others used riddles. Some used koans. But they pointed to something. It was not two minds that came together. No.

One would say this is the student and he asked the question. A question that to a Zen person or "master" does not make any sense. Like, "How are you doing today?" Or, "Good morning." And the other said a koan: "My heart is beating." Or something like that. These are not separate. These are one. One mind. Enlightenment and ignorance. One mind. Harmonizing together, and going through.

So, we are here. What do we realize about our lives? How did I really get here if my life is not really my life but rather the life of others? Why is my name—a limited view—so important? Why can it not be forgotten and the name of life itself arrive? Why is my name so important? This limited view. So the question is: Who brought you here? Who brought you here and what did it bring here? What did it bring here? So that your life is sitting right here and nowhere else in the universe. And you have no answers. Your answers will sound to the Zen master like they don't make any sense. "I came here to become enlightened." Why? "To sit." You were sitting at home. Everything—why? Who brought you

37

here? Forget the why. Who brought you here? And what did it bring?

And with that, thank you.

"When 'good' and 'bad' disappear, things can be as they are."

> *When you use "good" and "bad" to describe people, they cannot be who they are.... [H]ere your life is respected as it is. Whether you are "good" or "bad"—whatever you may believe. That life, as it comes through the door, is respected.*

Earlier today, I was talking to a person and they were telling me about good and bad; right and wrong. Good days and bad days. The things that they did not like and the things that they believed they liked. What should be here, and the way things should be. A separation or dichotomy—a delusion.

And they said something about the world—about how cruel it was. And they said something about morals and ethics—about how people should be good, not bad. Some rights and some wrongs. The way things should be.

I told her that none of these things exist in the world. They're not out there. All of these things exist in you—

because of your separation. There is no "world" out there. There is only your belief about the way it should be. Then I asked her, "If there is no world out there and all of these things exist in you, or are delusional within you, who will be kind to them? Who will take care of them?"

Then she went to her god. She said, "God" or whatever. I said, "What does he use on 'bad' or 'evil'? Does he push it away? Cast it out? Or does he use kindness, wisdom, compassion? Does he turn the other cheek, forgive, and love?"

Who will take care of this dichotomy or separation that is in us? So I said, "If you take care of the world within you, it will disappear and be as it is. None of those names would be on it."

So, we have two different things arising—we will call them "forms"—to go through. We will use the Eightfold Buddhist Path: Right Understanding, Intention, Speech, Action, Livelihood, Effort, Mindfulness, and Concentration.

These too are forms. The good and the bad—harmonizing and then going beyond them.

We talk about "sunyata"—emptiness. We say "form is emptiness" and "emptiness is form." Yes. So we see two things—emptiness and form. When both of these disappear, then what do we see? Things as they are. Or, is it even "things"? It is "suchness" ... "as it is"—beyond the labels and the titles. A teacher once said, "When will you realize there is no good and bad? There's just the way things are." One cannot exist without the other.

So, the young lady loved the good things, the right things—she wanted the world to be at "peace." She did not like the bad things, the wrong things, and the unpeaceful world. I said that if she had both these things in her and she let them both go—yes, let them go—things could be as they are. When you use "good" and "bad" to describe people, they cannot be who they are. They lose their naturalness. They become morally right, sophisticated, very clever, very sneaky.

They do all kinds of things "for" something. Yes. Kids do things that are very, very nice—so that they may receive. Yes.

So I did something good. And if they do something good, they expect something. Things cannot be the way they are.

In Taoist philosophy, when we abandon limited views such as "good" and "bad," "right" and "wrong," things go back to their true nature. This happens when there is no tampering with it, through manipulation and the different things we use. So, when we bring peace or we neutralize both energies in ourselves, then the world is neutral.

I told a person that if they can bring this to the world then they are fit to help others—to lead. Yes. They are fit to help others—to lead. Not discarding the delusion of bad or the delusion of good. But using these tools to awaken your true nature, as you are.

Sensei used to say that here your life is respected as it is. Whether you are "good" or "bad"—whatever you may believe. That life, as it comes through the door, is respected. He also said that it was respected to the point that in this moment, the exact moment of the breath, he had no wishes for it to change—only for it to be exactly as it is, without tampering with it by using morals and ethics. For some reason, these two that come in—"good" and "bad"—dissolve in the water of compassion. And they become one. And go beyond.

So, here we are. Good day, bad day. On our jobs. Talking to others. Things are not going quite the way we believe they should be going. But yet and still here we are. So somebody asked me if I was discouraged, and I said, "No. I want to see what's going to happen." All week, just a series of karmic events taking place. Yes, my life is very interesting. From ghosts in the car that turn the windshield wipers off—they only come on sometimes. To the furnace blowing up Sunday at the board meeting (it was cold, too). To all different things happening. This series of events. One cold day the car wouldn't start. Just a continuation. My life is very, very interesting. And I said to myself, limited views do not have the answer for these things that are happening. They are limited to discrete events—this one here, and this one here, and this one here. What do you do with these limited views? Meanwhile, I am noticing infinite possibilities. Noticing wisdom and compassion from the other shore as I enter into this karmic path. Bringing kindness into this karmic path. Smiling and saying, "It's okay. This is great!" Then others appear. Fixing the furnace—doing this and doing that. Amazing things appear right there in front of you. Not knowing where it is going to come from, but entering into it—knowing that this is beyond good and bad. Who cares about a furnace? It is about others, infinite wisdom and boundless compassion.

So we went down to the furnace place to get a motor and I run into a guy behind the counter and we have a big talk. He brings conferences to Cleveland. His name is Louie. I said, "Louie, you work here?" He said, "Yes." And he went and found a part and said he would give it to us for $80. Yes, "others." These things that seem to be tragedies bring about others that bring joy to one's life.

My life is very, very interesting. I don't know what's going to happen next. But since I'm here, why not jump into it? Don't be afraid. It looks like it is going bad. But jump into it anyway.

So, here we are. When tragedy comes, or something that seems to be not quite right—why not jump into it? Why not bring infinite wisdom and boundless compassion into it? If you do not, who else will? Remember that these things do not exist out there, only within you. Don't attach yourself to the furnace. You are interdependent, but the furnace is not here for you; it just does what it does. So it isn't that you have a bad karmic nature, or that things are going wrong, or that the furnace is there to freeze you. It only does what it does. So, one could say, "I am honored that it was there for the time that it was." Conditions are constantly changing.

And I think that will be all of my dharma talk. Thank you.

"While you are trying to become something, your true nature is arriving here and now."

> *One time I came in here and I sat down. And I looked. And I breathed. And all of a sudden the bell struck. And time had disappeared. The floor had disappeared. And I had experienced something. Every one of my sittings after that I wanted to go back to where that was. I had met the Buddha right there in the greatest sit of all. Now, I needed to kill him, and just keep going. . . . If you are trying to get to a place that the mind has said is great, kill it and just keep going.*

My teacher once said that everyone has the nature (or, he may have said potential) to become a Buddha or to be awakened. I would like to call it the seeds of enlightenment and say that everything has that seed to become enlightened. Both those that are seen and those that are unseen. I ask myself: The things that are around me—the conditions of my life—do I distort their enlightened nature by my viewpoint of subject and object because I am not enlightened? So, for example, I see trees as just things, animals, whatever. And I say, "Yes. They have the nature to be enlightened." But perhaps they are already there and it is just I who do not know what enlightenment is.

My true nature does not struggle. From the heartbeat, to the breath, to when it is time to go to sleep or eat. All comes naturally. It just arrives. So, I sit breathing with heart beating and hunger comes. But because I am not enlightened, or I haven't awakened, I do not eat. I would rather just have a bag of potato chips and keep on going. I have places to go and things to do.

So, do I view the world, or the things around me, with an unenlightened mind like this? A mind that is not awake—looking for something.

Here I am, looking at the world. And I am looking for something that my teacher said I am already standing in. Yes, I am dying of thirst. I hold on to the suffering of my life—in memory; in other things. Holding on to these things and not seeing the truth or experiencing the dharma. My life arrived right here this very moment. Just like every star that is in the sky and every blade of grass. It is in the right place. Yes. Yet still I do not arrive with it. I remain scattered all over the place.

All the things that are around me make my arrival in this moment possible. Why? Because they do what they do.

Yesterday, I was talking about the oranges and the apples. The orange has no limitations because it does not want to be an apple. Once it decides it wants to be an apple, then it will have limitations. Because it is trying to become something while its nature always arrives here and now. So, I am always trying to be something: Enlightened, a Buddha, an intelligent human being, a good person—yes—good husband, good employer. But I am always trying to be something. Instead of moving back into my nature like all of the dharma says—back into my nature.

Taoist philosophy talks about things that move back into their nature. Whatever they are, they are still looked after by the Great Mother. But my fear, and my ignorance, brings me out of my nature. So sometimes, once in a while, I may be amazed about what arrives in my life.

Earlier today, I told people that I once lived in an 8 x 14 room. I told them that before that I had a house in Cleveland Heights and a car. Then things went bad. We shall call them bad. They took a turn. And I became homeless. I stayed with people. But when you become homeless, you are never homeless. You can always go to the shelter. In another text it says, "I have already prepared a place for you."

I did not want to step down into that shelter, that hole in the wall, that garbage can. But something says to go that low, because when I send whatever it is I send down from above, no one will see it except you because everyone else is looking for something else. No one will see it. And they will want to know, "How did you get to the Cleveland Buddhist Temple? How did you get to these places?"

So, in a certain philosophy it talks about lying low. When the conditions change, you should have no preference where you go. Like water, it flows. But most men do not want to go there, but you should. No one else wants to go there. It is like hell and it is where you are needed at. And then all of a sudden, people are astonished. "What happened to you? You changed."

Conditions are like the struggle of coming up a mountain. Sensei always talked about that—struggling up the mountain. Now, in struggling up there you do have flat parts. It isn't hard all the time in trying to get to the top. And he talked about the fact that in the West they try to conquer the mountain while in the East they try to become one with the mountain. Going to the summit and looking out and saying, "Wow." Yes. Looking out and seeing it. But Sensei also said that this is as far as most of us will go because we will go back down the mountain. The ones that say "wow" when they see it and then step off into it, for them the things that were down the mountain disappear. Suffering, ignorance, all of it disappears stepping off into it.

One term for it is "shinji"; another is "faith". Now, one will ask, "How do I leave what is down the mountain?" I know I made it here. I'm feeling great. And now I can deal with it. I have peace. The job, the career—now I can take care of all of that. Yet these are all beliefs that remain the cause of suffering. But jumping off into it—it disappears. Arriving into this oneness. Jumping off into what words cannot express instead of going back out.

So, we would sit and sensei would say that after the sitting we should be quiet. Stay off in it. Instead of letting the senses take over. And expressing, and doing this, and talking about that, and yelling about this, and how great it was. That is like going right back down the mountain. He would say, "Be quiet. Stay in it. Stay in it."

All of these things do not mean what I am really talking about. It has something to do with something else. It has something to do with an experience. It has something to do with eating and digesting the experience—not just holding it in one's mouth. There is a Zen saying about a guy holding a hot ball in his mouth. It is about eating it, digesting it and letting it come out. Letting it go. In that experience. Not trying to hold on to it.

There was another teacher here, and everyone asked: "What do they mean when they say, 'If you see the Buddha on the road, kill him.'?" That is a very good saying. I've heard that before. One time I came in here and I sat down. And I looked. And I breathed. And all of a sudden the bell struck. And time had disappeared. The floor had disappeared. And I had experienced something. Every one of my sittings after that I wanted to go back to where that was. I had met the Buddha right there in the greatest sit of all. Now, I needed to kill him, and just keep going. So, there are all kind of teachers that will teach. If you are trying to get to a place that the mind has said is great, kill it and just keep going.

And I think that will be all of my dharma talk. Thank you.

"All arise from the same source."

> *One that is looking for wisdom and compassion will never find it.*

Earlier today, I was talking about conditions as if they were separate from our lives. The conditions that have arisen—these here—as if they are different from our lives. Talking about phenomenon or manifestations that are coming from the same source as our lives. Arising from the same source. I talked about the summer—dandelions blowing, park leaves blowing, all this coming from the same source. And I ask myself, "Who told me what is right and what is wrong?" Because, I don't like dandelions in the grass and other things that I do not believe should be there. Where is this suffering coming from and what ignorance brings it about? Is it rooted in the ego and the self—that it has a false sense that it creates? Or is it part of this phenomenon that is arising from the same source?

These conditions arise, and they have purpose. They make my life the way it is. By not using the words of right and wrong, or dichotomy or separation, they become nameless. So one would say, "Who are you?" And you might say, "They have not made a word that can describe this." This here has no words that can describe it. When we separate it we call it "dandelions", "grass", and on and on. But when it is whole, without our consciousness—this delusion or aggregate of consciousness whereby we perceive this thing, this form—when we do not use it, what does that form say? Or does it have no preference? It just grows or does its natural thing. Does it say, "The grass is here, so I must go there"? Or does it manifest in its natural state and live within itself. Its self depends on the conditions of all the other things that are around.

If I say "ought to" about the things that are around, do I "ought to" myself? Once I make the dandelion "bad," did I "ought to" myself? When I bring compassion and wisdom to these things, are they (or myself) allowed to be infinite?

Beyond this dichotomy of good and bad? Now "compassion" and "wisdom" are also limited words. What we are ultimately talking about goes beyond even those words. One that is looking for wisdom and compassion will never find it. Not by these words. They are pointing to something.

So I look at things in the summertime sometimes—the street, the grass, the trees, the sky and the clouds. Conditions constantly change. And I smile to myself and say that my life is moving in these conditions. The same way these conditions are doing. Not "another" winter, but *this* winter. This is the only one. These are the only conditions.

So, do I see myself as more than a year, or a week, or a single person? Or do I see myself as a changing part of all these conditions—beyond infinite wisdom and boundless compassion. Beyond the dandelions. Beyond the flowers that are dying. Beyond the apples and the oranges. Do I see myself beyond these things? And do I see these things as exactly what they are?

Sensei once said, "Things aren't what they appear to be, nor are they otherwise." Yes. Are they truly apples, oranges, and bananas? Or is that a limited view?

Earlier today I was talking to a doctor named Dr. Flemming. And we were watching a movie called "The Eye," where they put eyes in this lady's head and she started to see what the previous person had seen. So we'll call it a spooky movie. And Doc said that these people really have an imagination. The eyes don't see. Rather, it is the retina and all these other little things that are in there. And I said, "Yes, but isn't sight a phenomenon?" We are explaining what is there, but should we really be seeing this? And why is it like this? And why does it have all of these different things on it? Doc said, "We can explain that!" And I said, "I wish you would try." But isn't sight a phenomenon—an unexplainable event? And all the things that have arisen with sight.

So, with sight you walk around and you see dirt and grains of sand—all the things that have arisen. But isn't it a phenomenon? Doc would like to have a scientific explanation. I also said that since you're calling this idea nonsense, aren't most scientific experiments nonsense? They eliminate all the nonsense, and then they might come up with something.

So, can you hold these phenomenon beyond any explanation of them? Can you see that this sight that is here is a phenomenon arising from the same source as all other phenomenon and manifestation? What did a person in the '30s see? Did he see what I see? A person in World War II? All the way down. The Japanese in the internment camps? Everything.

You are the only one that is experiencing this life, this sight, this phenomenon. Isn't it unexplainable? No words can tell you what it is. I don't care if they use "retina" or whatever other words they want to use. No words can tell what it is. And all of a sudden, this life moves on and everything that it saw and registered—poof—is gone. It happens one time. Never happens again. People say, "This life is not amazing to me." They are lost in their explanations: "Well, it works like this, goes like that, does these little things like that, and let's get rid of the dandelions, get the grass nice, get an edge and do our little things, do some creating, whatever." But never looking, never studying what we call the dharma as it is. No.

I would ask, even when we cut the grass out there due to city ordinances or whatever, when you go to a field that is not cut and the grass grows high and you look at it, do you say, "Wow!"? All the different blends that are in there. Did they arise from the same source? And who says what is good, what is bad, what should be there, and what should not be there when it appears right in front of my face? When dandelions appear right in front of my face, nowhere in the universe will they appear quite like this except right here. But I say, "They shouldn't be here. They are messing up the landscape." In this ignorance, what causes the suffering? Because once I get rid of them, what happens? They come back. What causes the suffering? You will look at it. No other place that it can be just like this. Yet, I believe it is wrong for it to be there. Yet there it is. Ignorance will cause the suffering. Yes.

Another person asked me whether I liked being there with them. And I looked at them and I wouldn't say anything because to me it was not a question that could really be answered since I was right there with them. That word was so limited to the conditions that brought me there. Even the things that would be put into "dislike" made it happen. That word would be "sunyata." But yet and still we do need words. And I do believe a day ago I said one should be very skillful in using words because they cause a karmic path and suffering.

Another person I talked to was talking about their family and everything as "the enemy." She used the words, "they fixed me." And she was mad at them—"they fixed me." And that word can be used in two or three ways but she was using it in a negative way and she was going to get back at them because they "fixed" her. But yet and still, her conditions—whatever they did—have never been quite like they are now. So, the skillfulness of words, how we use them, is—I don't like to say important—but they may cause suffering or they can be used to point and go through.

One day I was sitting, and a person was there and the same questions came up, something like, "Do you like being here?" Or something like that. "It's a nice day." Or whatever. And sometimes when I'm just sitting, I just like drinking the tea or the coffee and maybe just a little quiet just for a little while before the conversation starts, before anything starts.

I was looking at the Tao Te Ching, and it talks about staying still till the moment of action. And, I ask myself, "What is the moment of action?" You can watch tigers and different animals and they may lay dormant for a while and then all of a sudden their stomach growls and they may do something. They may need to go to the bathroom or they may get thirsty. The moment of action. Very simple life. Cooking preparation, whatever. But can I stay still till the moment of action or do I need to create something to get out of my boredom.

And I think that will be all of my dharma talk.

"Your life is in your hands."

> *[D]o not worry about dying. What are you doing with your life right here? You can go on and die right after this breath. Go on and die. Do not worry about it. But this breath, what are you doing with it? Isn't life interesting? Your life, in these conditions.*

Not long ago there was a class here and I asked them: "Do you find your life interesting?" Some said yes, that they found their life interesting.

Our life is more than just our life; it is the life of others. When others act naturally, our life does not go the way we think it should. That is what makes our life interesting—this constant change; things on their karmic path. That is our life. Yes, we are connected to these conditions. So, our life is interesting.

Who got up this morning and said, "Wow!"? Yes, Buster, my dog, even said, "Wow! Snow feels funny. This is very interesting." [Laughter.] I walked around, scraped windows, got ice off things, let the car run and heat up. One may even say that these things are taking a toll on my life because, "I have to be somewhere!" But these things say this is where I have to be—even though I don't like it. This is where you have to be—infinite wisdom and boundless compassion. One of my windshield wipers is stuck to my car and I have to be somewhere. But right here, this is where I am.

Some person will wake up and say, "Do you realize that your life is right here? Not where you believe it should be." So, life does not go the way I plan it. But yet and still it is interesting. Snow comes. It was raining and snowing yesterday and I asked, "When will it stop, so we can meditate in peace?" The weather made all kinds of noise. And it stopped when it stopped. It did not go with our time. It did not care about us meditating. [Laughter.] No, it stopped when it stopped.

Arriving into the breath, out of time, the gong will ring when it rings. You do not have to worry about it. That is one thing you will never have to worry about—the gong ringing, the rain stopping, or any of those other things. So, arriving in this moment—that is your life.

Sensei once said, "You don't have to worry about dying. When death comes it will surely come." So, do not worry about dying. What are you doing with your life right here? You can go on and die right after this breath. Go on and die. Do not worry about it. But this breath, what are you doing with it? Isn't life interesting? Your life, in these conditions.

So, one of the Four Noble Truths is that old age and death, once worried about, seem to bring about suffering. Trying to figure out a way to escape it. I have got to do all these things about it. Just suffering. Why are you worrying about something that isn't even here? When it comes, there is nothing you can do about it. Yes.

So, sensei used to fly a lot. He would say, "My life is in my hands." When he got on the airplane, he would say his body was in the pilot's hands. If the plane fell down, it would surely fall down. But, my life is in my hands right here. He would make a statement to the effect that there is no reason to worry about it. Enjoy your life. There is nothing else that you can do. Your life is others. So, arrive in each moment.

He would also ask, "How are you doing?" If you complained about your life he would say, "Don't worry about it. You're going to die soon." [Laughter.] In other words, shouldn't you be trying to live your life in the here and now?

So, he would make certain statements that seemingly made no sense. Why would he tell me that I am going to die soon? Why would he say to me, "What does 'okay' mean?" I didn't know. It was just a term that I used. I am just conditioned to use these terms without even questioning them—questioning the path that they set up. So, what does "fine" mean? Dave, you look sleepy. What does "fine" mean?

Dave: "I'm fine." [Laughter.]

What does that mean? What does "fine" mean? What do you mean? And he would point and ask, "What is happening in the here and now?" He might say, "I am sitting right here. My heart is beating. I am breathing." Direct. "Fine," he would say, is relative to something and he would try to get away from the relative position. There is something else that defines "fine." If I give both of you a piece of pie and one of you likes it and the other doesn't, what is the truth? It is the same piece of pie but the description is relative to whoever is viewing it. It does not hold universal truth. So, he might say, "When you walk in the rain, you will get wet." That is a universal truth. Meanwhile, you are sitting right there. No where else in the universe. No one is experiencing your life except you.

You may believe that everyone here understands exactly what I am saying like you understand it. But if you were to get together and go somewhere and eat sushi and have a little sake you will find out that everybody heard something different. You will say, "That isn't what he said. That isn't what he's talking about." But everyone heard something different because they are the only one living their life. And each one is on their own karmic path. And the conditions that are around them—the same conditions that you are in—are different for them. So, no one can help you. That's right. You can forget about asking God to come down and save you.3 Your life is in your hands. Driven by ignorance, you will be awakened sooner or later. I like to say that ignorance will bring about the waters of compassion. Sooner or later, you will wake up. My teacher even said, "The more the ignorance, the greater the awakening." Yes.

---

[3] **Editor's Note:** The Buddhist concept of "No God" may cause difficulty for one who is attracted to Zen but is also a follower of a theistic religion. There are at least a couple of ways to deal with this problem. First, one may simply ignore it. Zen can be understood as a form of "mind exercise", and a belief in "No God" is no more necessary to benefit from this type of practice than it is necessary to benefit from, for example, lifting weights. Second, one may simply keep an open mind about the word "God". To that end, one may ask: Which of the following is descriptive of a greater "God"? (1) A belief in a limited God that I am separate from and waiting for, and for whom I must use the label "God" to define "His" limits (i.e., "This is God, but that is not God."); or, (2) A belief in a God that is limitless so as to preclude any need for the label "God" (and thus there is no "God"), and where the only limitation or separation arises out of my perception as filtered through my "knowledge" of Good and Evil. Some scriptural allusions to this second view include: "There is one God and Father of all, who is above all, and through all, and in you all." Ephesians 4:6; and, "The kingdom of God cometh not with observation: neither shall they say, Lo here! Or, lo there! for, behold, the kingdom of God is within you." Luke 17:20-21.

"Drink in the dharma."

> *You say, "Things are not going the way I want them to. Others are making my life difficult. If they only did what they were supposed to do, I would be all right." What ignorance. They are doing exactly what they are supposed to be doing.*

When I was a kid we were drinking wine on the corner. We were about 18 years old—maybe 16 or 17. We used to sing songs from the Temptations and some old Motown stuff. And we would drink wine and have our hair tied up. And there was a young man that came there that used to drink wine with us. And then one day he came and had a tie on, a suit, and a Bible. That's right. And he was awake. "Reborn." And we looked at him as if he was crazy and went right back to drinking wine. I remember that as plain as day. He came bringing what he called the "Good News." For the ignorant. To pour the water of compassion. But the good news that we had was a bottle of MD 20/20 and Colt '45. [*Laughter.*] So, his awakening came and no one heard it. His life was in his hands.

Our awakening comes, and teachers appear all around, but our life is in our hands. No one makes you unhappy. No one makes you happy. You are beyond limited views. Yes. Arriving here beyond these extremes in the here and now. So, what are you doing with that? You have read enough, eaten enough, slept enough, made enough money, did a whole lot of things enough, had enough sex, everything—it is all there. Did any of it hold your attention or satisfy you? Or, are you still searching? When will you realize it? Waking up right here, beyond these extremes. Happy, unhappy, sad, whatever. Beyond these extremes. You say, "Things are not going the way I want them to. Others are making my life difficult. If they only did what they were supposed to do, I would be all right." What ignorance. They are doing exactly what they are supposed to be doing. Their karmic path makes my life interesting. To wake up to that is to let go of one's ego self and drink in the dharma.

We are like men up to our necks in water, dying of thirst. Drink in the dharma. Just out there, I do not know where I am going. I do not know what is going to happen. But I am here. In the breath. Conditions changing. Life amazing. Basically, too soon to bring a comparison to it. Good, bad, right, wrong—beyond all this. Constantly changing. Practice this: "It is too soon to tell." It is constantly changing. Seeing others, then oneself. Merging in others, then oneself. So, my life is not just my life. My life is basically beyond my ego self. When it sees, the ignorance sees, it is amazed. Yes. It is amazed.

So, what are you doing with your life? I have been to a funeral today. It snowed today. I walked Buster today. A bunch of different people came into my life. The whole point is that the things that have entered into my life earlier today are fading away. They are in memory. I can not really see them. I can not really tell you what they were wearing or anything else. But they have brought me to right here. If everything in my life is that impermanent, shouldn't I put my whole self into it right now? All of those conditions have left. Yes. Was I in them? If it is that impermanent—if it is slipping that fast…that transient, shouldn't I jump into it? Jump into it—it is constantly changing.

That will be all of my dharma talk. Thank you.

> **"Sitting in ignorance."**
>
> *I asked earlier if the snow out there had any trouble falling or did it fall effortlessly? Because of the conditions, the snow had no problem falling. Not one bit of trouble. The conditions were perfect for it. But I have problems because when I am in my beliefs I am not part of the conditions. If I was in these conditions, would I be like the snow? Falling effortlessly? Sitting effortlessly? Walking effortlessly? Chanting effortlessly? Yes. To awaken is to arrive in these conditions.*

Earlier I talked to a young lady and she was complaining about a coworker. I used the story of a person grasping and holding on to something and not letting it go in order for something else to come up. What they believe they are struggling with is impermanent and has a karmic path. Yet and still they hold on to it, not knowing that once it is released something new comes in.

Infinite wisdom and boundless compassion is all around us in many forms. It releases us from our suffering and brings us to the fact that our life is right here. No where else. Beliefs can say anything they want to say. But to wake up, is to realize that my life is right here.

I also used for the past week the snow and the ice that formed on the windows. With all the rain and ice that was on the windows, I was getting up and struggling to get it off and needing to be somewhere—afraid I could lose my job…lose a lot of different things—running late, and all those things. I was fearful and trying to hold on to something. But there is this truth that says that my life is right here. No where else. This is the dharma. This is my life.

I do not trust infinite wisdom and boundless compassion—Amida Buddha—that these conditions are perfect. Why am I not enjoying them? I am enjoying the belief that I have to be at this other place that does not exist. I have to rush, have anxieties and worry. Never coming back to the breath and enjoying that my life is right here. The ice that is on the window has made it possible. Yes. This is my life. So, why am I not enjoying it? Here there is nothing else to do except scrape the ice off the windows. Everything else is taken care of. That's right. It is very simple.

So, my suffering arises out of my beliefs. Beliefs are ignorance. I do not care how smart you are. Beliefs are ignorance. Infinite wisdom and boundless compassion—once I let go of these beliefs one would say I will be amazed at my life. How did I arrive here, at the Cleveland Buddhist Temple? Was it by my beliefs? Or, was it by infinite wisdom and boundless compassion? Let's make these things—this dharma—the causes and conditions.

I asked earlier if the snow out there had any trouble falling or did it fall effortlessly? Because of the conditions, the snow had no problem falling. Not one bit of trouble. The conditions were perfect for it. But I have problems because when I am in my beliefs I am not part of the conditions. If I was in these conditions, would I be like the snow? Falling effortlessly? Sitting effortlessly? Walking effortlessly? Chanting effortlessly? Yes. To awaken is to arrive in these conditions.

There was a guy who used to hold rocks and say they were him. Basically, they were ideas that he had—things that caused his suffering. These conditions are me—right here. But yet and still I do not wake up to it. Yet and still I have a "plan" for them. And they are infinite, these conditions. Yet and still I bring my thirst and wants and beliefs into them. So, I never see the dharma. I always have to be somewhere. I am always racing somewhere, always exerting energy that goes nowhere, bringing about old age, death and everything else. Exerting energy in a condition that will never happen the way I think it should. Life does not go the way I believe it to. Arriving into the conditions, my life becomes effortless.

I have a thirst that says that I am trapped in time and I am in a hurry to get somewhere. A lot of people have this hurry to get on with life, success, careers and everything else. But all of this is tied up to a life. But yet and still that life is right here. So, I ask myself, do others and the conditions make me suffer? Rain falls effortlessly, flowers grow, leaves bloom, birds chirp, water runs. Everything does exactly what it does.

Yet and still I struggle when I am in these conditions. So I ask, if my beliefs were extinguished—say, by the Four Noble Truths or by the Middle Path—if my beliefs were extinguished, where would I be? Right here. Where would I be going? Right here.

Years ago when I was trying to go somewhere, do something, be something—I was like an apple trying to become an orange. Doing all these different things to try and become something. I was always right here, in these conditions. The rest of it never was anything more than just thirst in the mind for things like money and power—placing value on things that are empty. Now, a person won't believe this, but money is empty. It is about as empty as diamond rings.

John and I were up at Severance Mall today and in one of the jewelry shops they asked us to compare two diamonds and tell them which we thought was the "Leo" diamond. John looked at them and picked the right one. I couldn't tell. But the diamond didn't care. Better yet, the diamond just sits there and laughs. Which of you are foolish enough to believe that I am worth $2000 and I am going to bring you happiness. Think about it. It is supposed to bring you happiness and be worth $2000. It says, "I am worth two months of your working life." And then we wonder why we walk through life empty. My beliefs bring about suffering.

We might ask, where did these beliefs come from? Are they part of the Buddha dharma? Yes, they are part of the Buddha dharma. A belief that says I am supposed to be somewhere else, when in fact I am right here, seems to be ignorance and wisdom working together, doesn't it? Once I awaken to this and go over it and over it I see that I always have to be somewhere but I am always right here doing this. Then one day I look around and say, "Oh, I am right here." It finally catches up. That these two, ignorance and wisdom, combine and create an "ah-ha". Something I can't explain. I look around and everything seems as if it changed immediately. But nothing has changed. This was always here. But these two say "ah". They go beyond emotions and other things. They go to a place—I don't like the word enlightenment—they go to this place that cannot be explained. And everything that was here changes.

How many of you have heard the saying that mountains are mountains, then when you sit a little bit they become more than mountains, then when you sit a little more they become just mountains again? What they are and beyond. How many of you have seen the ten ox-herding pictures downstairs? Read about the gateless gate? All these things that are pointing to something that cannot be explained. To these conditions that I live in here, they do not exist. But those that have done this practice, these chants, move closer. This ignorance moves closer.

If you don't think sitting in the temple is ignorance, then I don't know what you think it is. I don't know what you think you are doing. If you think you are going to be enlightened because you come here where all this ignorance is—enlightenment doesn't need this. You need it to be comforted.

It is man-made, pointing to something beyond. It is kindergarten. But it is pointing beyond.

So, here we are. And the infinite wisdom we sit in is all around us. Yet and still, beliefs constantly come up. So, when will we realize this life that we live is the only one? This life is more than what I think I see in the mirror. It is everything that I see, and it is infinitely beyond that. It is the seen and unseen—this life. And the "ah-ha" comes, not because I just see it, but because the unseen is there and it makes my life a mystery. So, Buddhism taught awakening to this mystery. Buddhism is to be aware that my life is right here.

Tim McCarthy said something that I truly agree with: The Buddha didn't teach what you believe he taught. He didn't teach any precepts. Nothing like the Bible—do not kill anyone, do not take intoxicants, no fornication. The Buddha did not teach that. These things are all man-made, imposed by those who thought they knew what the Buddha was talking about. They would go to the Buddha and ask, "Should I kill someone?" And the Buddha would say what common sense should tell you. But he did not teach those things. So, a lot of rituals that they use are not the teachings of the Buddha. The Buddha taught the Four Noble Truths and believed that if you put the Four Noble Truths into practice, you would come to your own understanding. Yes. He would say, "Your life is yours." And he wasn't going to try to put it into some controlled thing. "Your life is yours. So, here are some teachings to guide you—now enjoy your life!" But, as with most children (as Tim would say), people came and asked "Should I do this? Should I do that?" The Buddha says, "Leave me alone. Your life is yours. Here are some teachings. And with these teachings you will experience your life." By using these teachings, a person wakes up to words that aren't really the words—we will call it "kindness", "wisdom", "compassion". We will just use words like "others" and a whole bunch of different words. But these are not true words. And you won't wake up because you believe in precepts he did not teach—what you should do, or anything else.

So, here we are. With the Four Noble Truths, the Eightfold Path, the laws of impermanence, the laws of causation, the laws of interdependence—here we are. These are for your experience. Take these teachings and have your own experience.

The Buddha twirled a flower and Mahakasyapa woke up. Everyone has heard this story of the passing of the dharma. Did Mahakasyapa wake up to the flower? Or, did enlightenment see the flower—that there was no flower? What happened, that transmitted the dharma? Was the object—the flower—transmitted? Or was it in its emptiness—interdependent upon everything to even be there—beyond the flower? So, one sits around and sees all this and it goes through the mind which is registering everything. And we do Zazen, and we do chanting, and it is registering in the mind and we are trying to…what? What are we trying to do?

So, I would just say that when it is snowing outside, let it snow. Or, when there is ice on the windows, scrape the ice. Remain there, and life will be effortless. Right here—instead of "trying"—remain here and life will be effortless. So, are you trying to do something? Or, is life effortless? Breathe in, breathe out. As soon as I say, "count the breath"—it becomes hard. Trying to count the breath—one, two—making the stomach move. Have you sat there and started like that and then let it go till it was so faint that you barely know it is there. And then all of a sudden it goes away and there is not one word. No count. Yes. Effortless. Or, have you ever been like me—I sat one time and my asthma made it difficult to breathe. And then, I just let it go—and the breath came by itself.

That will be all of my dharma talk. Thank you.

"Are you enjoying your life?"

> *If we are truly meditating, if we are truly arriving here with this breath, why are we in such a hurry?*

Once my teacher asked me, "How are you doing?" And I said, "Okay." And he made a grunting noise and said, "My heart is beating." He went beyond "okay," to exactly what was happening that moment. We were doing zazen meditation and the question really was: What was I doing right then?

He also asked the students who were sitting there, "Who brought you here?" That is a trick question. Somebody said, "I am sitting right here." The rest doesn't make a difference.

My life is existing right here. One could see that it was obvious who brought me here. These conditions brought me here. Not by seeing, but by knowing the laws of cause and effect we come to realize that these conditions made this possible. So, my life is really because of others. I live in the kindness and suffering of others that made these conditions possible.

He would also ask, "Are you enjoying your life? Are you being kind to yourself?" Your actions around the temple will show this. How do you take care of your cushion? How do you strike the gong? How do you do gassho? Do you do it with the breath? Or are you in a hurry to go somewhere?

So, how do you take care of your life? Are you kind to your life? Do you act in accordance with an understanding of the fact that the sacrifice of others has made it possible for the cushion and other things to be here in this moment right now. Even beyond "this moment"—this life as it exists right here—and beyond that.

So, he would ask, "Are you kind?" Or, "Are you enjoying your life? Being kind to your life? Are you using wisdom and compassion in your life?" If so, then you may be responsible for others—your kids, family, whatever. I also frequently use the example of talking to a person who uses words, and I ask the question: "Are you skilled at it?"

This here is the only time that you can sit or do what you are doing. So why not slow down and take care of this here?

Instead of being in a hurry and saying I will get better at it some time in the future but right now I have things to do so let us just sit, walk, chant and get this thing over with, but at some point in the future I will be able to stay around and do things a little better. No. This is the only time. Now, we know that there is no such thing as "time." The breath does not care about time. Nothing around you has anything to do with time. This is the truth, but yet we relate all things to it. But the breath does not care whether it is night or day—so it is beyond time. And what we are doing is beyond time. Here, here, and here. Meditation is beyond time. But then why are we in such a hurry to go somewhere? If we are truly meditating, if we are truly arriving here with this breath, why are we in such a hurry?

So, here we are practicing this tradition—arriving here for the first time. Are we using wisdom and compassion? Are we kind? Are we here beyond time like the breath? Here beyond time as opposed to here with the mind. Here beyond time if we have sat long enough. Not with the mind saying, "I've got to be somewhere." Just here. So, in Zen they say when you walk, just walk; when you sit, just sit; when you eat, just eat. Work and practice are the same thing. This practice is not just an hour. It is not thirty minute sitting meditations. It is not practicing walking meditation for ten minutes. It is beyond all of these things. It is arriving right here beyond all those things.

One may come here looking for something only to find they have been standing in it all along. And all that happens is that they have an experience that is beyond time. But that experience has always been here. That experience has always been here. The only thing that keeps us away from it is ignorance. But that ignorance is also in that experience.

I once said to a person, "Did you have the opposite end of an experience?" I was going to use dichotomy, going to try and use words skillfully, try to talk about something that is beyond words. He had an extreme experience over here. Then he had the opposite. Both of them came together. They made up something. And then they disappeared. That something that they went through is beyond words.

So, we have an experience here that brings something that says I am looking at the clock, I have all this time around me, all these things are moving, the candle is getting smaller, everything is still in time. Yet skillful words go through this and arrive beyond these things. Just walking, just sitting, just chanting.

So, he would ask, "Are you enjoying your life?" And the joy that he talked about is not the word "joy." Most people relate joy to something that is good. But enjoying your life in the sense that I am talking about it includes all aspects of your life. So, it includes your having a cold. Do you have a preference between joy and no joy? Are you enjoying your life beyond the dichotomy of it? Are you enjoying this life? Jobs you do not like and things you do not like doing. Do you find these things interesting? Since your life is so situated and your conditions or karmic path places you right there. Do you find it interesting? Even the many things you do not want to do.

Or, are we going back to time? "I have to go somewhere. I have to do something."

I would rather go, hurry up and get something else. We can see this in the supermarket when you have two items and you go to the twelve item or less line and there is a person there with more than twelve items. Oh yes, we know "I have to be somewhere."

So, are you enjoying your life? How are you doing?

That will be all of my dharma talk. Thank you.

"Beware of your conclusions."

> *[T]he dharma has no conclusion. It is constantly changing and becoming revealed. . . . but you believe you are "getting it" every time you come and sit. What are you getting?*

The Buddha once twirled a flower while holding it in his hand and Maha-Kashapa was enlightened. Out of a whole crowd of people, Maha-Kashapa was the only one that became enlightened. The Buddha knew he became enlightened when he twirled that flower.

Earlier today, we were talking with people. And they asked why we sit when there is nothing to attain since all is emptiness. And I asked them how they knew that. And they said they read it in a book. They chant it and it is in the book. I asked them again, "How do *you* know this? It can't be nothing because everything points to it." And he could not really answer with anything other than what was in the book. The Buddha said, "Do not believe what I say. Take it and go through it and believe your experience." But the book says something and so he answers, "Because it is in the book."

So, why am I sitting if it is all empty? What is your experience? We look at it. We read sutras, chant, and have beliefs. And we have words for conversation. But when there is no conversation going on, what is there? Some people will say "sunyata"—emptiness. But that is just going back to words and conversation in the mind with yourself. When there are no words there, what is the experience? The twirling of the flower and beyond.

So, we believe because we say "ah-ha" and the words make sense that that is it. The end to the means. But the words are still there. The delusion of the words that we read in a book. We say, "I got it! I understand!" But did we go through the words? When there are no words, what is? What is your experience?

To tell you the truth, I do not believe he sat long enough. Yes. Or, as Reverend Ogui would say, "He came to a conclusion after studying." Yes. And the dharma has no conclusion. It is constantly changing and becoming revealed. But he came to a conclusion of what was there.

Soon, they will be celebrating the Enlightened One's birthday. They will call it Hana-matsuri. And they will tell stories about it. They will tell about Heaven raining sweet tea. They will talk about the Seven Steps, the Four Directions, the pointing to the Earth and Heaven. They will bring meaning to it. They will ask, "Where is the Buddha?" And kids will point everywhere. But it is here, inside. They will always say, "Look in the mirror. It is here." Where is the Buddha? They open up the box for the kids and the kids see a mirror. Where is the Buddha? Is the Buddha the mirror of life without words or separation? Just look. And then go beyond that.

So, would it illuminate you? What would be the experience without words? Where is the Buddha? Standing in it and looking without words.

So, we sit, walk, chant, and analyze using our computer. Analyze words, put them in place, and get somewhat excited, "Yes, I'm getting it!" What are you getting? You walk right out of the temple, get back in your car, turn on the music, go do whatever—but you believe you are "getting it" every time you come and sit. What are you getting? Then we talk and we say one thing one day about a subject and then after we talk we think and more stuff comes to that subject and we move our thinking. The subject is getting good. Something new comes up and we think we are breaking through. "I'm really starting to comprehend." No.

So, what is the experience when there are no words? Twirl the flower. Did he see the flower? What is the experience? Everyone else saw the flower and said, "What the hell does that mean?" But Maha-Kashapa became awake. So, did Maha-Kashapa see the flower? Or, did he see the dharma—and beyond even that word.

And that will be all of my dharma talk. Thank you.

"Difficult is it to hear the teaching of the Blessed One."

> *The flowers are blooming. The tree has blossomed. These are words. But can you hear and see the dharma that is beyond these words? Or do you just see that the flower has bloomed?*

One can say, "The flowers are blooming." There is constant change. The tree has blossomed. Right there, right in front of our face, the conditions have changed. The impermanence of things seems as if the old has had its period and passed. Something new is constantly arriving. Yes. "Old" and "new" can be a dichotomy, but moving into the old is still something new. So, here we are, arriving in these conditions—new fragrances and a different experience. One never recognizes his own experience because he is too busy doing other things, but things are always constantly changing. Not the large changes that we notice with our eyes, ears and nose. Beyond these three—one change.

So, a person will ask: "Can you hear the dharma?" Since you were born in this human birth, can you hear the dharma?

But they are not talking about hearing by these ears or eardrums, or the smell and the taste of it. Can you see it? Not when it has already happened. This has already happened. Yes, the flowers are blooming, but it seems as if the mind and the senses are very slow because by the time they say the flowers are blooming, they have already bloomed. So, one may say: "Can you see the dharma? Can you hear it?"

One of the sayings here at the Cleveland Buddhist Temple is: "Hard is it to be born into human life, now we are living it. Difficult is it to hear the teaching of the Blessed One, now we hear them." In this saying, we hear echoes of the words that the Buddha taught—in parables and in the Four Noble Truths. And he broke these words down, but that isn't what he taught. He asked: "Can you hear it?" These words point to something.

Sensei Ogui once said something about a finger pointing to the beauty of the moon. All people have beliefs or, we could say, traditions. From Christianity to Buddhism to Taoism to Hinduism to Islam. All kinds of beliefs—including atheism. These are fingers pointing to something. He would say: "Go through the finger and experience what is there. Do not get wrapped around the finger and argue about the finger." All things are pointing to something. The flowers are blooming. The tree has blossomed. These are words. But can you hear and see the dharma that is beyond these words? Or do you just see that the flower has bloomed?

There is something that says: "I have sat here in zazen." Yet it is still just words. But what is it that has sat? Beyond what we think we see walking in kin hin and everything else we do here. One says: "But, I am awake because I have sat." Or they may say: "What was that?" Seeking that which is covered up by the words, conceptual ideas and different things. Going beyond what we see in sitting, chanting, and walking.

A person once told me something about a desire they remembered. And they said what the desire was thirsting after. And I asked them: "You experience the desire. You experienced what it was thirsting after. But did you experience what made it—that desire? Or was that outside your senses?"

One goes so far to get what one wants. But they don't experience the dharma, or the truth. Once they have this desire, this thirst, they grab for things. Since they don't know what it came from, or what made it, they write on it whether the experience was good or bad and things start to break into a dichotomy—into two different things. But it only came from this One—The One. So whatever it was, because of ignorance it was already enlightened. Just like the flowers and everything else.

Mahakashyapa simply looked at a twirling flower and we are sitting here looking at form. Computers in the head are talking to us in terms of concepts and everything else. They go down to a part in the Heart Sutra about the Five Skandhas—the aggregates. That no eyes, no ears, can sense this. But they don't go past this—no eyes, no ears, no feelings, no touch, no consciousness, no, no, no. They don't go past this. That is the thing that said: "I have a desire or thirst. I am chasing after something." But it never asks: "Where did it come from?"

See the flowers blooming and coming out of the ground. Know about the seeds and go on and on. But there is a point right there that the five skandhas, the aggregates, know nothing about. They cannot find it until they are extinguished. Practicing the Four Noble Truths or whatever path you may take—they cannot find it until they are extinguished. And then there is no word for that one thing. Yes.

So, that will be all of my dharma talk this evening. Thank you.

"Things are not what they seem to be, nor are they otherwise."

> *[D]o not look for great things in life or plan for great things. Move to the breath, and the conditions will provide the mystery in your life. Then you will be amazed.*

I grabbed the wrong pair of socks. They look like Buster ate them up. I have a dog in the back and he likes to eat socks. I also have a cold, a scratchy throat, I am dizzy, and a whole bunch of other things. But my life is right here. One could say, "I am grateful that such events have happened to bring my life here." That is what I always say. Are you feeling good or bad? It does not make a difference. Your life is here. So, go beyond these extremes. There is no other time for you to experience your life except right here in the present moment.

I want to use the saying: "Things are not what they seem to be, nor are they otherwise." So let me ask you, what do you see up there? [*Pointing to alter.*]

Student 1: "An alter."
Student 2: "Brightness."
Student 3: "Offerings."
Student 4: "Apples and oranges."
Student 5: "Fruit."
Student 6: "Apples and oranges."

Things are not what they seem to be, nor are they otherwise. We chanted the Heart Sutra[4] and it said something about form being sunyata: "Sunyata is form. Form is sunyata." Things are not what they seem to be, nor are they otherwise. Does anyone know what "sunyata" means?

Student: "Emptiness?"

Yes. "Nothing." "Empty." It is empty of the labels that we put on it. Yes. Basically, you could look at it and say, "phenomenon." Take the word and its meaning away and what do you see? No description captures it. But it is also not

---

[4] Please see Appendix II.

otherwise than what it is. Things are not what they seem to be, nor are they otherwise.

So, does anyone know what we mean when we walk around and chant the word "mu"?

Student: "Nothing."

Yes, it means "nothing" or "no self." So we walk around chanting the word "mu." When chanting and harmonizing with the sangha, bringing your whole self to it, you will hear one voice and then even that will disappear. So eventually there is no separate self walking.

I ask myself: "Craig, why were you having trouble walking if there is no self walking?" [*Laughter.*] Yes, my knees hurt, I was cold, my shoulders hurt, my voice is scratchy, I was trying not to cough. So why am I having so much trouble walking? Because while things are not what they seem to be, they are also not otherwise.

How many of you had trouble walking today?

Student 1: "My foot hurt."

What about you?

Student 2: "No trouble."

No trouble? So, you didn't look out the window while you were walking? You didn't get distracted by the cars going by? Didn't look at any of the pictures on the wall?

Student 2: "Okay. I had trouble walking."

[*Laughter.*]

Anyone else?

Student 3: "I lost my balance a couple of times."

Yes. It seems as if when we are not *trying* to walk we walk very smoothly. We never even notice it as we are walking in the park while talking to somebody. But when we bring our attention to it, it seems like we can't walk. So, these are practices. Because a lot of us believe we have awakened and come close to that point of understanding because of what we read in the literature. We have some understanding intellectually, but that is not really understanding. Yes. These practices are not what they appear to be, nor are they otherwise. They are waking us up to this self that is here *trying* to live life, instead of living life.

How many of you are trying to live life? Trying to make a life for yourself? Planning for something great that is going to happen—some futuristic plan? This self has already conjured up something for the future. Yes. This great self. So you are *trying* to live life.

Yesterday at the sitting I asked: "How many people are here trying to be good or better people?" And there was a couple here, and the woman raised her hand. And I told her: "Then you have already stated that you are bad."

Then we sat, and I asked the question again. This time her husband raised his hand. And I said, "That is great! Who, if not you, will take care of the 'bad' self that is here right now? If no one is there to bring infinite wisdom and boundless compassion to the bad, who will be responsible? Who will take care of it?" Then the woman said: "I should have put my hand up the second time." [*Laughter*.] Yes, the words change—they are not what they seem to be.

So, in your life there are things that you do not like. Dichotomies. From sitting, to colds, to everything else. To the position that you are in here. But who will bring compassion to them? Knowing that these conditions are impermanent and are moving on to something else, if you take care of the minutia the rest will fall into place. All you have to do is return to this breath. Just this one.

So, who had trouble sitting? Yes, because the time was great—thirty minutes. But if you would have returned to this very minute, just this breath, and realized that is all you are going to sit—one breath—then the rest would have just popped right into place.

So, one says: "Do not plan great events." I have seen them come in here and say: "I am going to sit for hours. I'm going to do Buddhism." Then they keep looking at their watch saying: "Damn, when is this going to be over?" [*Laughter.*] So do not look for great things in life or plan for great things. Move to the breath, and the conditions will provide the mystery in your life. Then you will be amazed at your life. Move into this one breath and these constantly changing conditions and you will ask: "How did I get to the

Cleveland Buddhist Temple? Where did it come from? My life has changed, but it appears here—nowhere else."

I have seen a lot of people who come here and when they are here they do not want what is here. So they make plans and go seek elsewhere. This is what they call thirst and suffering. They arrive in infinite wisdom, compassion and kindness and yet they do not want to be where they are. They want something else that is created by the delusional or suffering mind that says: "If I can only get this other thing, then my life will be great." Things are not what they seem to be, nor are they otherwise.

I know this person right now that is looking for a Hummer. They saw another person with one and now they want one. But these two people are like apples and oranges. The person I know is not making a lot of money, but they saw this girl with a red Hummer and now they want one. But things are not what they seem to be. Because from the house to the Hummer car note to the gas to the insurance to everything else, you—because you are here and want something in the future—will create your own suffering. Your life, for some reason, will be unmanageable. You won't be able to do anything with it. It will be all out of control.

But once we sit, returning to the breath, it seems as if infinite wisdom and boundless compassion settles everything and things go back to normal. The repo man comes, the bills come in, and guess what? All of a sudden I am back to where I was before. And you know what happens then? I want something else. And the whole process, the wheel of dharma, just keeps turning and turning and turning.

So, when will you realize that your life is right here, and there is nothing here to want? Things are empty. All possibilities are arriving in this emptiness. Changing and moving on. Constantly changing.

And I think that will be all of my dharma talk. Thank you.

"How are you?"

> *Things are constantly changing. The flowers are dying and the trees are blooming. . . . . Probably you are trying to become enlightened when there is no such thing. . . . To go through is to go through is to go through. . . . It is the kindness of meat that leads the vegetarian to vegetables.*

There were people here Sunday, and they heard Socho Ogui tell the story of the birth of the Buddha—pointing in four directions, taking seven steps. They also heard him say: "Things are not what they seem to be; nor are they otherwise." They also heard: "Your mother wanted a perfect child, but you came out." So, Socho Ogui has taken all my best stories. Of course, he gave them to me first a long time ago.

[*Laughter.*]

There is another story he tells. He went to a retirement home and when he came in all the people were just sitting there. So he asked them all to say: "How are you?" So that is what I want you to say—"How are you?"

[Sangha: "*How are you?*"]

Then he would tell them to say it louder. So, say it louder.

[Sangha (louder): "*How are you?*"]

Yes. And what he was saying was: Not others, but you—how are you? Is your heart beating? Then he added to it: "I am grateful."

[Sangha: "*I am grateful.*"]

The meaning of: "I am grateful"—what does it mean to you? Are you looking at the limited self?

I am grateful. The incense is burning away. The flowers are dying. The conditions are changing.

There was a movie, "We Were Soldiers," with Mel Gibson about Vietnam. And the general on the other side—since you have to have two sides if you are going to have a war—the general on the other side said he was grateful for those that had died and those that were about to die. He was grateful. Others make our lives.

How are you? I am grateful for the ones that have passed down such traditions and sacrificed so many things. The flowers are dying and others in our lives make us say: "How are you?" My heart is beating and I am here—right here—because of others.

These conditions are constantly changing. So instead of clinging to the flowers as they were this past Sunday (they were beautiful this past Sunday), instead of clinging to such dualism, say: "Yes! They are as they are." Things are constantly changing. The flowers are dying and the trees are blooming.

So, something moves on to leave a space for something new to experience a present experience that has already changed. Each breath is like that. My life—right here. My life—walking. Because of others. I am walking and I am grateful. I am sitting and I am grateful. When one looks at all the conditions in one's life, one will be grateful. The rain is falling and it will stop. The clouds are moving. Things are passing on. This experience is whole. Birth and death arrive at the same moment. Go beyond both of these conditions. Go beyond. Go to life itself. Beyond the two extremes—the dichotomy. Walk right here. One step at a time. Then, once that step is over, it leaves the next step. The next breath. These steps and breaths never come back. Just like this here. It is never going to come back.

Every year that I have been here, there has been a hanamido here with flowers. They always look like the same kind of flowers. It is the same order every year. I can show you the order form. It is the same thing every year. But they are passing—never to come back. If they were to remain here never changing, would you say they were beautiful? Some people would say: "Please go somewhere. Let something else appear." Then when they were gone we would talk about how beautiful they were.

Sensei told a story about a man that came to him who had a problem with adult movies. He said, "Sensei, I cannot stop watching adult movies. I am having this problem. What can I do?" Sensei grunted, and then told him to go and buy a whole bunch of those movies and enjoy himself. Watch them eight hours a day for a week. So the man did and at the end of that week he said: "I don't want to see another adult movie again. I am so tired of the same thing." He went through it. Now others would have said: "Stop!" But this is not correct. Just keep on doing it. Go through. Go through. Go through. Eat all the ice cream you want. You will find out. So sensei would say: "Enjoy yourself." Go through these things.

We hear stories about the baby Buddha. The children look at the statue and they don't think it looks like a baby. But there is a story about the baby Buddha and it is a representation of what it truly means. And the story talks about a child that makes a cry right there when it first comes out of the womb. It gets smacked on the butt and makes a cry. And that is the statement: "My life is the most honorable one." That cry right there, that is the statement that it makes. Nowhere else does that life exist except right here. That is the baby Buddha, right there. That smack. That first cry. It yells out that my life is the most honorable one.

The story of the baby Buddha also tells of how the Buddha spoke of relieving the suffering of all sentient beings and took seven steps. There are six senses. Man uses five and has a sixth sense—we call it intuition. But there is a seventh one that when he walks into it he is walking out of delusion. He is fully awake. Boom! Out of delusion. Yes. He is fully awake and aware. So we have that cry that says: "I am fully awake. There is no delusion here." So, here he is—the baby Buddha. The one that will expel suffering. So the baby Buddha is right there [*pointing to members of the sangha*], right there, right there, right there. The one that will expel suffering. Now, you might say God is going to come out of the heavens and help you out. But you can forget that. This is your life. So, you are the one.[5]

We also read something that says: "Hard is it to be born into human life, but now we are living it. Difficult is it to hear the teachings of the Blessed One, but now we hear them. If we do not deliver ourselves from suffering in the here and

---

[5] Please see footnote 3, page 66.

now, there is no other time that we can do it." So who are they talking about?

There are two things that are here. One thing is the ego self in the delusion that there is a true "me." The other is the one that came here and with a smack took the seven steps. Yes.

There is another saying that says there is a being that moves in and out of your senses. Your heart is beating, your lungs are taking in air, when it is hungry you have to feed it, when it is tired you have to go to bed, when it has to go to the bathroom you have to carry it. This being that is moving in and out of your senses, that has no preference, who is it? Did we bring it here to sit, or did it bring us?

Probably you are trying to become enlightened when there is no such thing. Buddhist priests use the word all the time, but there is no such thing. Reverend Ogui, when he was teaching the Zen classes here, would tell us there is no such thing. Then he would tell you all about enlightenment and we would say: "I thought you said there was no such thing." And he would say: "Figure it out." But there is no such thing. To go through is to go through is to go through.

We are living in the kindness of other things that are disappearing. We are living in the kindness of things that we do not like. From people to careers to everything that is out there. Even to the taste of foods—we are living in the kindness of others. It is the kindness of meat that leads the vegetarian to vegetables. If you prefer cherry pie to apple pie, it is the kindness of the apple pie that helps you. The kindness, even of the things that we don't like, helps us.

People go to coffee shops and look at different cups as if the hole that holds the coffee is different. This is delusion. When will we bring wisdom and compassion to the things that we do not like as well as the things we do. When will we wake up, cry out at the smack, and take our seven steps to walk out of delusion knowing that this is our life, right here, and everything makes it happen.

And that will be all of my dharma talk. Thank you.

"Do not seek enlightenment."

> *Do not look for the idea of enlightenment or an awakening or to wake up. Do not look for this idea. You will always fool yourself that you are there. Just use this form and one day you will be amazed.*

One may say: "I am pleased to see you." Another saying is: "I am grateful to the things that are changing—moving on, never to express themselves in this manner again."

Someone earlier today told a little lie, we will call it that. They said they would love to sit for an hour-and-a-half. Yes, they would love that. But the conditions did not allow for that.

Beyond the time that we sit there is one breath. In time, one breath doesn't make any difference. But if truly you sit for that one breath, then you will have sat far beyond that one hour.

The Buddha sat for 49 days but he awakened with one breath and the morning star. We talked about this yesterday and I asked: "Who awakened?" His name was Siddhartha and all his teachers from the ascetics to everyone else gave him different names. But when he awakened they said the Buddha awakened. Not Siddhartha or any of his other names. And he was a Buddha. No title and enlightened. No one label could fit on him. He passed through all these things in forty-nine days. All the separateness became one.

So when he awakened there was no one left to awaken. But when we awaken we still say: "David" awakens. Yes, that's right. You have a great sit and the floor disappears and lots of different things have happen and "David" or "Craig" was there to notice all these things. The delusion is still there, of a self to awaken. To be truly awake the delusion would have to be broken through so that there is no "me".

So yesterday we had some professional sitters here. They sat for 12 minutes and then they were awake. That's right. I believe one of them said his name was Charles. They sat 12 minutes and they were awake. They stopped counting the breath. They disappeared and the breath disappeared. The name of it and the mind that is following it. So, they have awakened to the absolute. And it only took them 12 minutes at a beginners' class. Yes. But I could ask: "Then why are you here?"

My teacher said: "Do not be fooled by your thoughts." Do not fool yourself. Your life is right here. To bring wisdom and compassion or to chant the words of the Nembutsu, the Heart Sutra . . . whatever. But bring it right here. Do not look for the idea of enlightenment or an awakening or to wake up. Do not look for this idea. You will always fool yourself that you are there. Just use this form and one day you will be amazed. One breath you will be amazed. It will come without effort using this form: Gassho, the chants, the Nembutsu, and all the different things that we do. All of a sudden, without recognizing it, it will be as crystal clear as the morning star. Yes. And you will not have to say, "I have awakened." Because I will not see anything except whatever that crystal clear star represented.

I also told them about a guy named Bodhidharma, the 28th patriarch of Buddhism and the 1st patriarch of Zen. He left from India and went to see the emperor of that day. The emperor asked: "I have built many temples in the Buddha's name, what merit is it?" And Bodhidharma said: "Nothing." And the emperor asked: "Who are you to tell me this?" And Bodhidharma said: "I don't know." He had no name.

So the awakened ones seem to have gone past any title that clings to them. They are beyond that. The awakened ones look at things without titles or names. They go back to their true nature—what they truly are.

When you look at the flowers you can say it is a beautiful arrangement. It is so lovely. And yet they are constantly changing. So at this stage you might say they are dying and bring emotions like the five skandhas, form, and perception do. But the awakened one doesn't even see them as flowers. There will be no title and they will drift back to their true nature on their karmic path.

So one may say: "I am grateful at the appearance of this as it moves on, knowing that my life is dependent on it and moving with it at the same time." Yes. Studying the dharma, from the candle to the incense to the car that just passed by to the things that are around—the movement—is to study the impermanence and interdependence of life itself. If you truly study it, you cannot say it is a "tree." You cannot use a limited word or view that is from the delusional self or the five skandhas that say it is a "flower." No. The awakened one has no view—he is beyond "flowers." His view will be unlimited.

I went to see another friend, he is a muscle-bound guy. So I go to his basement where he has his weights. He is opening up a gym. Today we discussed a limited view created in time with the five skandhas and the ego self and I said: "You see the limited view of where you want to go and what you want to do."

Life itself is all around you but you never see it because you are always looking at this limited view and how to get to it. And you are always getting to it. And when you get to it and you are there it isn't what you want it to be. Then you wonder what else you can do. Then you look back and time has gone by and you wonder what is wrong with all the others around you. And the whole point is that you never saw them. You saw only this limited view. A delusion that is in time—over there—when your life was here beyond all titles. Infinite. Infinite and beyond all titles. No limits. No limited view. Things constantly moving, changing, and becoming.

So, seeing the limited view is like a dream, while life itself—unlimited possibilities in the present breath moment—has slipped past. You never experience it because you are too busy going to that limited view.

Teacher once said that most of us will die with our eyes still closed. He was not talking about the eye that is looking at that limited view but the one of infinite possibilities. Would you believe that a person can sit in that limited dream their whole life—trying to get "there"? In the end there is only regret about everything that mounts up—that life was not fair. But he never saw what was arriving into every moment.

So we are here sitting, walking, chanting. How many of us are enlightened by sitting on this cushion? Teacher would say that you can sit in the here and now, chant in the here and now, walk in the here and now, do work-practice in the here and now, but do not look for enlightenment in the here and now. Do not deceive yourself. And he would say that if you do these things you will be amazed at your life. And that word that people are looking for will only be that you are here—no where else. No labels. Here, where everything has gone back to its true nature.

These flowers will not be "gladiolus," they will go back to their true nature. Beyond limited words. That limited word is just like me looking for it, missing everything around me because I'm looking for these glads.

And that will be all of my dharma talk. Thank you.

"Just sit for twenty years."

> *We chant "mu" while walking. When you start you will hear many voices chanting mu. Then one day you will hear only one voice. Then one day after that you will chant mu and you will not hear one voice because there will be no one there to hear one voice—there will just be the Nembutsu. You will have moved past the dichotomy of: "Form is sunyata; sunyata is form." There will be no need for these words, which are for the limited mind. This is moving into infinite possibilities.*

Welcome.

One day we were sitting here and there were new people here. One of the new people asked me: "When will I be able to sit like you or Reverend Ogui or the others that I see sitting here?" He said that he was unable to focus and was always distracted, always moving, always antsy. Even the flies that would come in would distract him.

I said to him, "I have been sitting here for twenty years." He said, "Yes, I understand. But when will I be able to sit like you?" And then he went through all his difficulties again. And then I repeated, "I have been sitting for twenty years."

The twenty years do not have that much significance. But the breath that sat does. The focus on the breath.

One day he was sitting and he was swatting at the fly. And I said, "Leave the fly alone and just follow it." And he did. Wherever the fly went he followed it. And the distractions of the cars and the birds disappeared. The fly was part of the dharma.

We have read in the books and in the sutras about things that will wake us up to our delusions and attachments. So, the dharma is what was waking him up.

For twenty years I sat over there, my back hurt, my knees hurt, I couldn't focus. I experienced everything he did. So I said, "This is very interesting."

Can I tell you when it will happen? You will know when that breath comes. In that breath will be the conditions and one thing is that they will never be like mine. They will be the only conditions weighed by nothing else except that moment.

Yes. So my saying that I have sat for twenty years says nothing except: "Sit down."

My teacher once talked about, and in Jodo Shinshu they talk about, deep listening. Submerging yourself deep in the Nembutsu, the chants, the sound of mu—deep listening. If you are sitting and the water is running at Euclid creek, practice deep listening. Go beyond the sound of the water. Go beyond the sound of mu.

There is another person that comes here, he has been coming recently. And he said that he had the experience of walking around and chanting mu with the sangha and he could hear only one. And I said, "That's great. Keep chanting mu. Until you go beyond whatever it was that heard one. Just keep chating mu."

So, deep listening is not with the ears. Deep listening is deeper than what the ears can pick up. It is the whole being listening to the dharma. The whole being—the dharma and it as one—and going beyond.

We chant mu while walking. When you start you will hear many voices chanting mu. Then one day you will hear only one voice. Then one day after that you will chant mu and you will not hear one voice because there will be no one there to hear one voice—there will just be the nembutsu. You will have moved past the dichotomy of: "Form is sunyata; sunyata is form." There will be no need for these words, which are for the limited mind. This is moving into infinite possibilities.

So, these forms that we are doing help us to break through. Chanting mu. Practicing deep listening. Chanting up here on the alter. Seeing the alter, but going beyond what we believe we see there. All of a sudden, it will not register. There will be no words—just a stare. And then all of a sudden it is back—there it is.

"Just sit."

> *We are not here to perform, but rather just to sit and hear the dharma and let it come in naturally. Reverend Ogui would ask: "Who is showing off?" When you are sitting, walking, chanting—are you showing off?*

So here we are at the Cleveland Buddhist Temple. You take this dharma talk out and talk to someone about it and they may think you are nuts. If you go out and meditate in formal posture on the bus, they will really think there is something wrong with you.

There is a story about a master and his disciple. And they were in "plain clothes"—they had taken off their robes. And they entered public transportation and the master sat like everyone else but the disciple sat in formal meditative posture. And once they got off the bus the master hit the disciple and asked: "Why are you showing off?" What was the reason for that, instead of just arriving with everyone else?"

Reverend Ogui used to say that if you once did transcendental meditation, we do not need you to levitate here—just sit. If you did visualization, we do not need little things running around—just sit and count your breath. That is all we need. Don't show off. Just sit, walk, and chant. Be useful by sitting. Just sitting and walking and chanting. He said that by doing this without showing off you are useful to others because they do not need to wonder: "How do I do that?" They can just sit.

We are not here to perform, but rather just to sit and hear the dharma and let it come in naturally. Reverend Ogui would ask: "Who is showing off?" When you are sitting, walking, chanting—are you showing off?

So, there is a point of no-self. Sometimes Reverend Ogui will be here and he will make a grunting noise, look at everybody, say a few words and say: "That is all I have to say." Then he would leave. "That is all I have to say." He would also point to a senior student and say: "If you don't like what I have to say, complain to him." Then he would leave.

So, here we are and a person might ask: "What kind of dharma talk are you going to give?" Why should I plan my dharma talk? There is no reason to do that. Just sit and whatever the dharma is, there it is. So, sometimes you see something that has an agenda: You are going to see this and that! So there is an expectation of what is going to take place. Here, there is no expectation. What kind of dharma talk am I going to give? Maybe it will be one that has no words.

So, if we are doing deep listening, do we hear the dharma? Or maybe you hear the noise that is coming out of my mouth. Maybe you are trapped by that noise—asking whether it is right or wrong, agreeing or disagreeing. Or are you into deep listening? Are you beyond the comparisons for right and wrong?

And that will be all of my dharma talk. Thank you.

"Who will be kind to your life, if not you?"

> *In each one of us there is a good man, and it is the teacher of the bad man. In each one of us there is a bad man, and it is that good man's charge. When they come together they will make that complete circle and there will be a little bit of each in each one of them. Who will take care of the "bad man" in you, if not you? Who will stop the suffering in your life, if not you? Who will invite the child out of the closet, and into life itself?*

Recently, I talked about something in the Tao Te Ching. I also talked about "deep listening" and asked if you could hear the dharma. And I talked about something that we hide and that what we hide we believe to be "sinful". In the Tao Te Ching it says something about a good man being a bad man's teacher and a bad man being a good man's charge. This may be translated differently in different texts.

In Buddhism we believe that we suffer because of ignorance, which we may call the "bad man". Most of us would like to be the good person that is the teacher of the bad man. Yes, we would love to be that teacher. We read the book and then say, "I am going to teach you something about the Tao Te Ching or Buddhism." Others may say we suffer because of ignorance and that we are afraid of old age so we try to avoid it by exercising and doing all sorts of weird things. Almost as if we are trying to escape it by trying to get somewhere. We also suffer from sickness and use a lot of different things—remedies, cough medicines, washing our hands to try to keep the germs away—to avoid sickness. We suffer from death—another form people would like to avoid—so we make a Heaven and different things. We also suffer from loss and gain—fear of losing the ones and things that are close to us. The very thing which in infinite wisdom and boundless compassion moves on.

This suffering causes things such as greed, hoarding, grabbing hold of, controlling—all sorts of things to try to keep things intact and not lose them. We would call this an unnatural act in the face of conditions that are constantly changing and beyond these extremes of good and bad, right and wrong, death and birth…whatever. So, we create suffering for ourselves by the actions that we take—actions that show that we have not woken up. There are also other things that we learn when this life is born here—from morals to ethics, to doing things "right", to receiving things if we do the right thing. These things could be said to be not quite true. But we have learned these things.

So, must of us would like to do things right. Be the right person and everything else. These things have been created. But there is something else that has come up that goes against morals and ethics and is outside societal values. It is a part of nature that is natural. In the Tao Te Ching they have it and it is the Yin-Yang symbol. In each one of these symbols there is a piece of the white and a piece of the black. But these symbols are put together as one. Yes.

In human relationships and experience we would like to separate these two things. So, I will show you my best side. I will show you the creation of Craig's mind. I will cut my hair, take a shower, put on my best clothes, be very polite and everything else. But at the same time I tell the bad little kid:

"You can't come out today, I'm going to put you in the closet because I don't want anyone to get a glimpse of you because I know exactly what you are going to do—you are going to act up." And he goes into the closet. Then I suffer. He has not been invited in.

But yet it states in the Tao Te Ching that a good man is a bad man's teacher and a bad man is a good man's charge. Zen tells us that there is nothing here except you and your karma. But when we read this from our western perspective we see what they call a dichotomy, we see a split, we see two things. But I do not believe the Tao is talking about two things. I believe that the Tao is talking about one.

In each one of us there is a good man, and it is the teacher of the bad man. In each one of us there is a bad man, and it is that good man's charge. When they come together they will make that complete circle and there will be a little bit of each in each one of them. Who will take care of the "bad man" in you, if not you? Who will stop the suffering in your life, if not you? Who will invite the child out of the closet, and into life itself? Simple teachings, but yet and still so complicated. The cry of the dharma.

And everything that is being talked about is symbolism. It really isn't what it says. There is no bad man or anything like that. But it is symbolic of two forces and an ignorant delusional self ignoring one of them—trying to be something that does not exist. Without both of these forces harmonizing together things cannot be natural.

So, how many people do you know act unnaturally? All you have to do is look at a baby and then look at the dining room table of someone who likes everything in order. All you have to do is look at them and watch nature as it does its thing. We imitate nature and try to make it better. We do not understand where it came from—yet we would like to make it better. We do not see that it is beyond that which we say is better—that our views are very limited.

So, one would say that there is only one. When will we break through ignorance and bring the oneness in the closet to the table? What will we use to do this? Meditation? Zen practice? The Four Noble Truths? The Middle Path? The impermanence of both things? The interdependence of them? What will we use?

So, here we are, and I would like to know: Who is the teacher of the bad man? And why is the bad man the teacher's charge? You must ask yourself this. Even sit on it. And you will find out that both of them originate from infinite wisdom and boundless compassion. And if the Tao translates out to the "path," then both of them are the path. And if "Te" translates out to "virtue," then both of them have virtue. Yes. So, why are we not bringing our whole selves to this?

I said in the beginner's class that you should sit and have no preference. The breath has no preference. Whether you are a good person or bad person. Whatever your beliefs are. Whether you are sick or well. Whether you are in jail or free. Whatever your sexual preference. The breath has no preference. It arrives with both of them. Maybe it could be the teacher of the bad man and also the charge of the good one. With no preference. Arriving into it.

So, the question is: Who will be kind to the things that they do not like? Who will invite them into life itself?

And that will be all of my dharma talk. Thank you very much.

"Beyond form, into the Sangha."

> *When the sangha, the Buddha and the dharma become more important than "my" accomplishments, then there will be effortless action.*

If you were to come through that door right now, entering into the Temple, can anyone tell me what foot would come in first?

Student: The left.

Which one would go out first?

Student: The right.

Right would go out first, and the left would come in first—are you sure?

Student: No.

If you were to walk up to the altar, which foot in Jodo Shinshu would come up first? Can anyone tell me? How many steps is it to the altar? Which foot goes back first as you back away from it? Can anyone tell me?

Student: It's up to the individual person.

Actually, there is a form that is used in Jodo Shinshu.

Does anyone know how the instruments are played? Basically, it is a drop. A wrist drop. Drop, drop, drop. So, let us go on.

If you were to enter into the Temple, which foot would you use? Which is the enlightened foot? Even the hint doesn't give it away, does it? Which side is the candle on the altar on? Ah, you see it is on the right side. So, that is the foot of enlightenment, wisdom and compassion. Impermanence is over here on the left, representing the body and the delusional sense of permanence. So, one would come in with the right foot—wisdom has brought you here. And when you leave, leave the wisdom foot in and bring it out last. Yes.

There are three steps to the alter: dharma, sangha and Buddha. One, two, wisdom. Impermanence comes up from behind in the form of the left foot. Hold your hands chest high and as you bow point toward the Buddha at forty-five degrees. Come back up, hands down, impermanence departs in the form of the left foot followed by wisdom in the form of the right foot. One bow is a forty-five degree bow and the other one is a thirty-degree bow. You didn't know that did you? Oh, that makes me a pitiful excuse for a teacher. But what is your awareness of what you see and hear—the strikes on the gong, the spaces in between, the ringing of the instruments. I did a pitiful job today—I struck on top. There is a certain sound when you hit it in the right place.

So, the drop, the sittings, all of these are forms. How should one come to these forms? If you bring the self you are tense and rigid. You should come with your breath and breathe. How many of you breathe when you do anything—sit, walk, chant? How many of you breathe to keep the same beat or flow with the breath or the rhythm? And then letting the breath go and just letting the rhythm and the breath and the body move together with no mind. Breath—step—breath. Starting off with the breath and then letting the breath go. Probably on the second walk around you are letting the breath go. Yes.

So, here we are at the Cleveland Buddhist Temple practicing forms. When I started drumming here I would be doing my thing and my teacher would just get up if I wasn't looking at him and get right by me and demonstrate the drumming. That is what he would do. He would come down from the altar and simulate the striking of the gong. To show me how to breathe. He would come here and look at the incense and it wouldn't be burning right and he would show me how to lay the incense sticks. Now, I am lazy and my knees hurt so I don't get up as much.

And there were different rules about the sutra books and how the Temple was supposed to be laid out. All of these were forms to be practiced just like tai chi or sitting. To be practiced till you could do them as easily as twirling Chinese meditation balls in your hand without them touching while you read a book. It just went that way. And then beyond that way. Yes. Beyond that way. The balls and the hand are moving at the same time. No balls, no hand. Beyond that. Mind is empty and one is free. So, all of these are forms—

even the lighting of the candle. Then some day you will extinguish the incense with one sweep of the palm. There will be no need to shake it. So, what is your awareness of the arrangement of the things that are around us?

There was once a group here that was in a hurry to get somewhere so they worked their cushions real fast, jumped up and bowed real fast, and asked, "What's next?" I said that is just like eating all your food and then asking what is next. The answer is nothing. That was the meal. You should have stayed there a little longer.

Yesterday, I talked about the trees that were moving. They were dancing in the sky—just blowing. I asked people that were looking at them whether they saw what made them move. You see them moving, but you never see anything else that made them move. So, what makes it move? What did it move with?

Everybody talks about studying the dharma, the breath, the self, and everything else. Everybody talks about being interdependent with these things—moving with these things.

Most people would say the muscles in the arm are moving the hand when you strike the drum. But if you breathe it seems as if it is free and drops by itself, bringing you back to the breath.

So, my teacher once said: "Do one thing. Just do it. Then add this and this and this." So, some of us will sit, get the back straight, rock, get the oval mudra perfect and by the time we get it we find out we haven't taken a breath. We forget to breathe. Then we will breathe for a while but then it will cut off because we are trying to get our focal point perfect. So we have this erratic sitting—doing this, doing that. And someone will say, "Let it go." Just go back to the breath. Do not worry about the focus. It will glaze over eventually. If you have your spot, you can hold it. But eventually you will let it go and arrive here. Arrive with the sangha.

Yesterday, or we would say other breaths ago, I talked about the individual and the accomplishments of the individual. Their accolades and how they get it all right in these conditions that do not care about right and wrong. When will the accolades and the accomplishments of the individual disappear and become that of the sangha? Someone comes in and says, "Boy, Craig put these cushions together well. They are so straight." When will that disappear and instead they say: "I would like to sit in this sangha." Or, someone might say: "Craig can meditate really well. When can I meditate like him?" I would say that I came here twenty years ago and sat over there and could not meditate worth a dime but I could not leave because no one else would move. The sangha made it possible for me to sit over there and do what it did.

We hear much about individuals, but never the sangha. But yet and still we read that we should take refuge and faith in the sangha and the Buddha and the dharma. Not in Craig or his accomplishments or anything else. Then I find out that there is no suffering. Here I am. I have a sangha. When the sangha, the Buddha and the dharma become more important than "my" accomplishments, then there will be effortless action.

So, here we are at the Cleveland Buddhist Temple. And at the beginner's class I rarely state my name. It is just not that important. When we used to come here years ago we never really talked and I really did not know anyone's name till we went out to eat after a sitting. The name was not important, but everyone looked forward to practicing with the sangha. Names came later.

So, here we are. We use our titles and what we do. Everyone that comes in through the door sees people all around and does not even notice that there is no one here except you and your karma. The sangha is your karma. There is no one else here. So, when you have faith in it, or take refuge in it, there is no you. When these conditions are your life, then you have entered into the sangha.

So, here we are and often someone will ask if there are any new people here, as if there are some old people here. And the new people may stand up and say their name but the next week—who knows. You do not really know them anyway. They are just part of the sangha. As one sits it seems as if their names are not important. Their names are only important for conversation. No names are important in sitting, walking, chanting, whatever we do. And then when true meditation comes in, the mind does not say "sit" or "chant" or "walk"—it just does. There will be no names. There will be less words. And all of a sudden, there will be infinite possibilities.

So, here we are tonight, experiencing the sangha.

That will be all of my dharma talk. Thank you.

"Does the dharma need your 'happiness'?"

> *I am . . . in exactly the right place in my life to receive the dharma. . . . But yet and still I would like [things] to change so I can be happy, so I can find the delusion of "happiness", which does not exist. You know why it does not exist? Because <u>that</u> is out there. Yes. Because <u>that</u> is there and nothing else exists.*

Not too long ago, I was talking about the dharma. Most Zen people would tell you that they have nothing to teach, so there is no talking. Rather, there is just being one with the dharma and waking up to a truth about the way things truly are.

There were people here not too long ago and they wanted to be happy but they wanted other things to make them happy. Yes, they wanted better grades in school, better boyfriends and girlfriends, better conditions, better cars, houses, taxes, everything. Their happiness depends on others.

The dharma is permanent while delusions are constantly changing. So, they wanted these things that are on their own karmic path to stop their lives and come and entertain them so that they could be happy. They wanted others to stop their lives and entertain them. Do certain things to make me happy. Cooler weather, hotter weather, dryer weather, wetter weather—it does not make any difference.

Are you hot? What happens when you are hot? You sweat. That is the dharma. Yes, we used to sit up here in 90 degree weather and others would want to bring fans but Reverend Ogui would say: "No. When it is hot we sweat. Just sit." Do not wish for it to be cooler. Sit in the heat. When it is cold do not wish for it to be hot. These things that happen are so impermanent that they are constantly changing.

So, why don't we bring our whole selves to these conditions the way they truly are? Because we want to be happy. We want this to change so I can be happy. Can that change? Can that thing I am pointing at change to make me happy? It is supposed to be empty. There is nothing there. And everything out there is on a karmic path. It is going somewhere. It did not come here for my beliefs or my entertainment. Better yet, it is part of me—interconnected. It is doing exactly what it is supposed to be doing, including the cars moving and the dogs barking.

There was a person here who said that if the cars and the trains weren't moving and the dogs weren't barking and the birds weren't chirping then they would have a great meditation. Everything would be quiet and they could really meditate. And I said to them: "Do not wish for anything to change to make your life better. Not one thing." There is no such thing as "better." All beliefs such as this are delusional. Your life in the here and now is the cars moving, the dogs barking, the birds singing, the wind blowing and everything else. Why do you thirst for something to be different? Why do you thirst for a delusion that does not exist? Some would say: "As soon as things get better I will enjoy my life." So, they wait for a better day. How many here are looking for better days? Nobody? You know that is a trick question. [*Laughter.*] But really, we are all looking for better days.

So, the class that was here not too long ago, I looked at them and said: "Yes!" A lot of them were young and they were waiting for better days—to get away from their parents, to graduate from college, to get their house and wife and BMW and everything else. They were waiting for better days—for it to be "mellow" outside. We talked about this and I said to them: "Okay, well then let us not waste our breath on these days here. Hold your breath until a better day comes that deserves your breath and your heartbeat." When we compare things—this day against yesterday, this day with some future that doesn't exist—we are trying to compare two different things when only this day exists. And this day, right here, this moment, this breath, has never existed before. It cannot be compared with the breath or heartbeat of yesterday.

So, this is not the "better" day. It is beyond that limited understanding. This is not the day that provides happiness. This is beyond that limited understanding. Yes. This day, with one breath, has infinite possibilities without the self. The candle is getting smaller, the incense is burning, a different car has just moved past, there are different humming birds, the wind has just changed direction. In one breath, the whole universe has changed, never to happen again. And yet this is not amazing to people.

Yesterday, the class that was here did not realize that the leaves on the tree outside have never been here before. They thought they were the leaves from last year. They did not realize that those leaves have never been here before. Most of the people that were here had places to go and things to do. And they thought that they were in the wrong place in their lives. They thought they should be somewhere else—further along, happier. And I told them about the leaves that have never been there before—this is the first time they ever came. And they did not find that amazing. They did not even know about it. And I told them that each one of these leaves, when it falls, will never fall at the wrong time. They will all fall exactly when they are supposed to. And there are probably trillions of them in Cleveland. Yet not one will fall at the wrong time. But the arrogance of ego, or the delusion of the self, believes that I am in the wrong place in my life. Such billions and trillions of things have made this possible. And I am just like them—in exactly the right place in my life to receive the dharma. Its karmic path makes my life possible right here. But yet and still I would like it to change so I can be happy, so I can find the delusion of "happiness", which does not exist. You know why it does not exist? Because *that* is out there. Yes. Because *that* is there and nothing else exists.

So, here I am at the Cleveland Buddhist Temple. Conditions have made this possible. I have sat, walked and chanted. Cars have provided noises, dogs have barked, conditions have changed. And I am here. I have taken care of my cushion, bowed, did a whole lot of different things—all past, never to appear again and basically fading from memory. Yes. Some will say the sitting was painful, or long, or boring. But all of that suffering is fading from memory. Yes. By tomorrow, to use a delusional term, it will be just about evaporated.

Yesterday, I said I was going to give the same dharma talk today that I gave then. So, I remember that I said I would give the same dharma talk, but now I do not remember what dharma talk I gave. It is already gone. How did it come together? Maybe that dharma talk was connected to the conditions that were here then and those conditions have changed and that dharma talk will never appear again. That was a great dharma talk I gave yesterday. [*Laughter.*] Yes. This one is not worth much. [*More laughter.*] If only I could get back what I did. So, do you understand? This is the comparing of two things that can not be compared.

So, we arrive here, beyond likes and dislikes and dichotomy. Should we bring kindness and wisdom to these conditions? Can we stop depending on past conditions or future conditions? Should we free ourselves from them and rely on the dharma and these conditions right here—this breath? Should we sit or bring our whole self to this dharma, right here—since it is fleeting and moving on?

The Buddha woke up to a truth. They even say he went all the way back through his past lives. So, every possible scenario arrived in him in his forty-something days of sitting. Every one of them had a breath that had no preference, had a heartbeat that had no preference, had wisdom and compassion and kindness. Sitting right there, he had no preference, seeing every last one of them. Yes.

Have I sat long enough to have no preference? Whether it is hot or cold, a bad or good day. Have these delusions disappeared? Yes. Do I see that my life is right here? Has the kind and compassionate heart of the Buddha arrived here?

We sat right here. It was hot. I wish it was a little cooler. But the breath had no preference. Knees hurt. But the breath had no preference. I do not like what is going on. But the breath had no preference. Each one of these states had Buddha nature arriving and supporting it with infinite wisdom and boundless compassion. Yes. It is almost like the saying of Taoism, that the Great Mother nurtures all—takes care of all. Yes. That breath arrived here and in the midst of all the delusions that the mind was playing, it had no preference. It brought life, comfort, compassion, wisdom and kindness. Beyond these words—they only point to what was arriving as these delusional beliefs came up. So, since my life is sitting in the dharma, is it not too soon to tell whether it is too hot or too cold, whether this is taking too long and I should be somewhere else and so on? Should I not just stop, take a breath, look around and say: "My life is right here. And I am grateful to all the others that make this possible. One of which is the heat."

And that will be all of my dharma talk. Thank you.

"Does the dog have Buddha nature? There is no dog."

> *My sensei said: "You are hungry. Why would you buy a cook book? Why not just eat?" So, we are standing in water up to our necks dying of thirst. When will you drink from the water instead of trying to drink from a book?*

I heard this story on a television program, but someone else said it was written in a book. The story told of a wild bird that was flying and its wings froze and it fell and died. And the narrator said: "A wild thing will never feel sorry for itself." It would never feel sorry for itself.

When we sit, we sit in the heat. Yesterday I came out here and they had fans in the windows. I asked: "Who put these fans in the window?" And I told them to take the fans down. So, they put them back and we sat in the heat. Yes, there is an air conditioner or two back in the house where I stay. But rarely do they come on. When the dog is hot, I may turn them on, or when company comes. So, we sat in the heat.

A wild thing never feels sorry for itself. But sitting in the heat we want to feel comfortable. Yes. So we make air conditioners and fans. But yet and still, these things are also made from Buddha nature. We may call them "ignorant," but they are part of Buddha nature. To make these things, to cool off, just to sit in the heat again. These things that we make in ignorance are also the things that wake us up to the fact that it is surely hot when it is hot. Yes.

So instead of trying to escape something, the Buddha was wise enough to make something that seems to bring comfort but in fact brings us back to truth. When we sit in the heat, we sweat. When it is cold, it is truly cold. We cannot stay in the comfort of our delusional ideas.

Since the beginner's class uses a guided meditation I say: "Ordinary mind is the way." So, what is ordinary mind? Yes, if ordinary mind is the way—what is it? So, we looked at the flowers and the fruit on the altar and I asked them: "What are they?" Anybody know? The flowers, right there, what are they?

[*Student*]: "They look like carnations."

They are carnations. Color?

[*Student*]: "Red and white."

Red and white. Any other colors in there?

[*Student*]: "Blue."

Yes. What about the fruit? A person would probably say: "Apples." Yes.

Ordinary mind is the way. Yes. So, all of the things described: carnations, red, white, blue, whatever—what have we done by describing them? Once we describe we cannot have ordinary mind. Yes.

Has anyone ever heard of Mahakassappa? He was a disciple of the Buddha. And the Buddha twirled a flower without saying a word and passed the dharma to Mahakassappa. The Buddha also had a very close friend disciple, Ananda, but when the Buddha twirled the flower without saying a word it was Mahakassappa that was enlightened. So, ordinary mind is the way.

Does a dog have Buddha nature? Answer "yes" and you lose your own Buddha nature. Answer "no" and we will just say you are incorrect. So, most people find an answer in a koan book. And when the teacher presents the koan, those students go straight to that answer. But if the teacher then asks why they said that—they do not know. They just read it in a book.

Did the Buddha write anything? No. Well, who wrote all the words down that the Buddha said? Some people that were listening to him. Did they know what he was talking about? No, they did not know what he was talking about. They had to change everything so they could understand. They did not know what he was talking about but they wrote stuff down in a book that you are now reading even though the authors did not know what the Buddha was talking about.

What about Christianity? Did Jesus write anything? No. Who wrote everything? His disciples wrote down what he said. The way Jesus's disciples are described, does it sound like they understood what he was talking about? No, they did not understand. But yet and still you read all these things in a book written by those who did not understood. And that is what it is.

Ordinary mind is the way. Now, does the dog have Buddha nature?

[*Student 1*]: "Uh, Mu?"

Straight out of the book. Why did you say that?

[*Student 1*]: "Because that is what I read somewhere." [*Laughter.*]

Does the dog have Buddha nature?

[*Student 2*]: "Wu."

Does the dog have Buddha nature?

[*Student 3*]: "There is no dog."

Ah, there is no dog.

Does the dog have Buddha nature?

[*Student 4*]: "Mu."

Someone said there is no dog. Someone yesterday asked: "What dog?" Ordinary mind would never see a "dog." There is no such thing. Most of you said "Mu", which means no self. So, who is perceiving a "dog" or "flowers"? Why did the flower awaken Mahakassappa? What did he awaken to?

Was it the nature of ordinary mind that is beyond such things as "dog" and "flower"?

So, here we are in this mystery using our senses. And all the teachings have been pointing to ordinary mind. We go vast distances in time and space to find a book, read the book, and then go to a coffee shop or drink tea, in order to have a conversation about the book. Then we make up hypothesis and hypotheticals. So, here we are discussing the teachings of the Buddha and someone says, "if." And then they go into their hypotheticals. Then another says "but." And then we change things again. And then the conversation is over and we had a nice cup of tea, a beautiful conversation, and we go off thinking what a great thing that was. And yet everything we talked about came out of a book—delusional.

So, how many of you are "Book Buddhists"? [*Laughter.*] All the other ones have done all the investigation. [*More laughter.*] My sensei said: "You are hungry. Why would you buy a cook book? Why not just eat?" So, we are standing in water up to our necks dying of thirst. When will you drink from the water instead of trying to drink from a book? In a book we read words based on linear notions of time that talk about the Buddha as if he was 2000 years ago—as if this enlightenment is not always here. We use things such as history—5000 years, 2000 years, whatever. As if whatever it was went somewhere. Instead of being right here. So, a person will ask if there will ever be another Buddha. Not for the Book Buddhists. They are somewhere else still in delusion.

When you sit, why not go beyond that. As you breathe, one breath after another. Beyond birth and death and life. Someone might say that is impossible to do in the real world. It does not make any logical sense. I have to eat, I have responsibilities, and so forth.

We talk about things appearing and disappearing. We talk about things constantly changing. We talk about the mind that makes up scenarios of things that it is going to do later on that never happen. Yet, we are right here. So, why do we use the rationalizations and justifications that play in the mind of

"I have to get a job"; "I have to do this"; "I have to take care of that"; "I have to pay for this" and everything else, when you life is right here? Life is sitting right there. When will we arrive with less preconceived ideas and arrive into life itself? When will we do that? Preconceived ideas come in terms of names. When will we arrive into this empty? No "flower", no "dog". Just look at it, and go beyond.

Japanese tea ceremony. Monks come out and just look. People that sit around and have tea without conversations. Others in the monastery that walk past without comment. Cleaning without conversation—just work. But once I walk past my politeness says: "Good morning. How are you?" And I start to create things like "good morning" and "bad morning." When will we let these things go and just sit.

So, Mahakassappa saw the twirled flower and received the transmission from the Buddha. How did that happen? Another one wakes up to "There is no dog." It is a very, very good answer. But who is saying the answer? It still has the taint of intellect on it. Although it is a very good answer. One will sit there and that question may be asked and something outrageous may be said because the question does not make any sense. And someone may just say: "I am sitting right here." Or, "Life itself is right here." Others may say: "There is nothing here except me and my karma."

So, the teacher does not look for an answer to the question of whether the dog has Buddha nature. That is why the word "Mu" is there and "no dog" and "no self." The question eliminated both the dog and the person that perceived that there is a dog. So, you said there is no dog. Ah, you were drawn into the trap! [*Laughter.*]

So, my teacher would just say: "Go sit there." And then one day I receive this robe. And it was not based on anything I said. It was the way I picked up the striker, turned it, and made the strike. And then he said: "It is time." The flower was twirled and nothing else needed to be said. Now, I am not saying I am like Mahakassappa, but in that moment that is the way it was.

So, you sit and you read koans out of books and read the answers and yet there is still this separation. Nothing that disposes of both of them—the separation of dog and self—so as to bring an awareness. Number one—it is very hard to get rid of me. So, that is the very hard one. So, here we have koans. And the koan today was: "What are these to ordinary mind?" And if you said "flowers" and identified what is up there on the altar, then there is no ordinary mind. A mind that has morals and ethics and . . . what is your name?

[*Student*]: "My name is George."

And George. All born here. What about before you were born? Ordinary mind is: "Show me your face before you were born." Not "George." So, what did Mahakassappa do when the Buddha twirled the flower? What was out here is delusion. We already all know that.

There is a saying that says that when you practice Zen mountains are mountains; sit a little longer and mountains become more than mountains; sit a little longer and they go back to being mountains. Yes. So, what did Mahakassappa see or do that was beyond what was learned here. No words did he speak. I have this sense that it has something to do with ordinary mind. So, when you answer a koan by the intellect on the basis of separation of the self from what is pointed to—sit a little longer.

That will be all of my dharma talk. Thank you.

"Who is sitting?"

> *No matter what my beliefs or what I add to it—it can only be what it is. And that is beyond the labels and the words that I put on it. Every time I put a label on these conditions, I have separated myself from them.*

Did you explain to Buster that we were meditating? [*Laughter.*]

[Student]: "He was barking at his leash."

You see, dogs don't really care that we are meditating. [*More laughter.*]

So, you have come out in the heat and sat in it. Yes. Now, did you think: "I am coming out into the heat"? Did a thought come: "I am going to the Cleveland Buddhist Temple to sit and it is going to be hot"? Or, were you like the breath that just arrives here. Not saying that it is hot as if the heat is separate from you. The heat is me. Nothing out there says: "It is hot."

So, how did you arrive here? Did you arrive with a thought that you were going to be sitting in the heat—that it was going to be hot? Or, did we arrive and simply find these conditions and move beyond that separation.

I told you earlier to drink some water so you wouldn't dehydrate. I have sat here in 90 degree weather, 100 degree weather—just sweating. Usually we put on other t-shirts under our robes and just sit. The sweat goes away. Sit long enough and it dries up. Just sit. But the humidity doesn't go away. [*Laughter.*] So, how did you sit here?

Smelling the incense and feeling sweat run down your back or chest—how did you sit? When we sit beyond these "trickle-down effects," not noticing them, deep into meditation—is there the heat? Are we sitting in the heat? Or, are we sitting in the dharma or the truth? Beyond the words that can have a dichotomy about them—but rather sitting in the dharma.

I do believe I saw something today that said something about the conditions that will remain just like this and can be nothing other than they are. No matter what my beliefs or what I add to it—it can only be what it is. And that is beyond the labels and the words that I put on it. Every time I put a label on these conditions, I have separated myself from them. Yes. See, my name is "Craig"—when I put a label on, I am separated from you because you have different names.

Once upon a time, we came in the Temple and I knew no one's name. I sat just right over there, but knew no one's name. So, there was no separation. I just sat down. Whatever it was, it was just sitting right there. Then names started to enter and interests arose. So, instead of just sitting there and doing work practice I started looking forward to tea and cookies and I couldn't wait to go to the restaurant after practice and so on.

So, are you practicing this form, learning about the labels, and realizing that they are not quite true? When you are by yourself, who are you? Yes. Who is sitting? Do you say: "Your Name" is sitting? Does the thought, "I am going to sit" come in? Or, do you just sit? What happens?

So, one may be aware of one's conditions and what preconceived ideas come in and smile when these ideas arise and wonder: "When will these preconceived ideas go away?" So, the sitting is free. Then one may know who is sitting. The preconceived idea says: "Dave is sitting" and "I am going to sit." But who is really sitting?

Now, both of these things are here. Some may call it the nembutsu or the wisdom from the other shore that brings to consciousness at this level the idea: "Let's go sit." And the ego self says: "Craig is going to sit and do all these great things by sitting." When will the nembutsu or wisdom from the other shore become noticeable? When will it become noticeable? Then, we can recall the writings I talked about last week: "Do not take yourself too seriously"; "Do not lose your sense of humor"; "Do not lose your sincerity"—and they will be understood. Each word or combination of words is understood at different levels of consciousness. So, each of us is experiencing something different—even in this conversation here. Here you are, the only one experiencing whatever it is that you are experiencing. And no one else is experiencing this like you. The labels of words, the names of things that are around us and everything else. Including the belief that we are true Buddhists. We are hard-core Buddhists maybe. [*Laughter.*] Or, we are militant Buddhists. [*More laughter.*] We sit with no fans and no air conditioning. We are doing it just like they did 2000 years ago in India in 100 degree weather. Just sitting in it. No shade, no nothing.

So, here we are with nothing around except the noises outside, sitting in the heat. Yet and still we cannot create the conditions of the Buddha. We cannot create it. We cannot create the conditions of the Buddha. So, when we look at his conditions we will never wake up. So, we can read all his books and look at all his conditions many years ago and we will never wake up.

The Buddha said: "Do not believe what I say. Believe in the dharma." We read it in our books: "You are the dharma. Believe in the light. The light is within you, which is wisdom. Believe in nothing except the dharma and the light." But yet and still, we use a lot of words and we say that our given name is going to sit.

Who is going to sit? Is it the wisdom from the other shore that brings us here? The dharma? Is the dharma and the wisdom from the other shore and the light and the heat—are they all the same thing? It has been said that our true selves are beyond birth and death. So, are all these things the same thing?

So, here we are at the Cleveland Buddhist Temple. And I always ask: "Who brought you here?" So, I ask again, did you have a preconceived idea before you got here? And, who is sitting?

That will be all of my dharma talk. Thank you.

"Show only one face to all things."

> *There is a story about a mother that passed away, and the son that was looking for this mother. He believed that she was in Heaven because she was a "good mom".... But she was [in Hell] because she only took care of what she believed was hers. She never took care of any other kids or anything else that she did not perceive to be hers. Her son ate well while the other children nearby went hungry. He had the best of everything while other children had nothing.*

Everyone has a "great event" that is in their mind and that they are looking forward to happening in their life. They come here looking for a great event—enlightenment, or something that is big, to bring what they call "meaning" to their life. Shunryu Suzuki said there is nothing special. Yet and still, we plan for big, huge events. To the things that are around us they are very minute. But our perception makes them very big.

So, this great event that is going to happen—enlightenment, and all the big things that can be seen—I bow to. Yes, gassho. But the little things, I pay no attention to. The very small things—the wind, a bird that sings, listening to the water—I pay no attention to them. The unseen I also pay no attention to. While I am busy looking for this big event, my life slips right by. That is my life, slipping right by.

I take care and nurture this great event with all kinds of forms—from chanting, to writing, to sitting, to meditating. We do not believe that this is going on, but it is. It is in "enlightenment," it is in "waking up," it is in striving to become a "Buddha," it is in striving to become a "better person." But there is no such thing. The flowers tell us that. The things out there tell us that there are no such things. This is what it is.

So, here we are. Looking for this great event that is going to happen—from jobs, to careers, to peace, to contentment, to all kinds of words that we use to label a thing that never will happen. But we believe it is going to be a great event. The five skandhas are agitated or awakened by these ideas. Excitement comes in. The form comes out. I am going to get a raksu this week. And a Buddha name. Yes. This great event is going to happen. The Dalai Lama is going to come. And I will sit here and he will bless my beads. A great event! Something is going to happen. But yet and still, in every breath—the small, the unseen, the minute—moves right past. Life itself moves right past while I pursue my great plans never understanding that all of these parts are one—and never really seeing that the great event has already happened a long time ago. Yes. I am standing in it. It already happened a long time ago. But using words that were formulated after the event to describe it, I am looking for it in books that are written in words that came after the event.

There is a story about a mother that passed away, and the son that was looking for this mother. He believed that she was in Heaven because she was a "good mom." She had given him everything he needed—fed him, never hit him, educated him, taught him manners, etc. So, he looked for her in the realm of Heaven. And when he did not find her there he kept looking for her in lower and lower realms. Finally, he found her in the realm of Hell. And he wanted to know why she was there, since she had been a good mom. But she was there because she only took care of what she believed was hers. She never took care of any other kids or anything else that she did not perceive to be hers. Her son ate well while the other children nearby went hungry. He had the best of everything while other children had nothing.

There is another story about a person that went to the gates of Heaven waiting to get in. And his maker was there—we will call him the "Big G." And this person told the Big G of all the things he had done. How he had taken care of his family. How he took care of his job. How he took care of all of his things. How he respected the toys he got. How he praised God for giving him certain things and abilities. And the Big G looked at him and asked: "Did you take care of my sheep?" And this person's mouth shut. "Did you take care of my sheep?" Not just the great events—the "white sheep"—but the "black sheep" too. The ones that don't like you—did you take care of them? Did the mother take care of the other kids—particularly the ones that did not like her? Or, did she only take care of her kids?

So, here we are. We take care of our great events. But yet and still, for the minute and unseen that support our lives we do nothing. Not even an acknowledgement with a gassho. Yes, we sit, we walk, and we chant—but all in anticipation of a great event.

So, when will we be kind to the small, the minute, the unseen? The things that are here now. Yes, they do not need gassho. They do not even need to be acknowledged. But they are here.

In readings it will say: "Show only one face to all things." But I guarantee you the great event brings about another face—a smiling face.

So, here we are at the Cleveland Buddhist Temple. Letting it go. Just walking. Just sitting. Nothing special. Just chanting. So that one day the Nembutsu, or Buddha, will flow through every thing. The minute as well as the great as well as the unseen. And even the word "one" will disappear. If the word "one" disappears, what do we see the flowers as? Since we already know that the word "one" automatically implies "two." What do we see the flowers as? Would they have a name? Or should we say they are simply as they are? Not great events, not small events, not big events, not minute events, not even the unseen events. Rather, life itself—interdependent and beyond limited views such as great, small, or unseen. Life itself beyond oneness and everyday suchness. Others use the word Tathagata or "Thus." Beyond any label that can be put on it—boundless life and compassion.

So, here we are sitting, walking, chanting. Are we looking for great events? Are we looking for something to happen? Why are we here? One might say as it does in Reverend Ogui's book: "I am sitting right here." Yes. Not saying anything about anything else that is around, but simply that my life is right here. And if so, then my life is connected with the seen, the unseen, the great, the small—any word, and beyond that word. It is right here. It is impermanent and constantly changing. Am I paying attention? Or are the five aggregates, the five skandhas, active in the forms I practice and my perceptions. Add a few feelings and something great is going to happen. When will this cease? They say this part is suffering. In this excitement there is also fear that it may not happen. There is also doubt. But it is still there. There is so much in there that generates it.

So, here we are. Right view, right meditation, right speech—what are we doing? Did we come here because we believe something was going to happen?

In the two stories, I am told that I cannot be focusing on "mine." I will have to empty out everything and become others. To become others is usually to abstain from causing a karmic wake that disturbs their nature. We believe that this karmic wake comes via our actions. But while I believe I am being "good," my thoughts continue to judge others. In one book it says that as a man thinketh, so he is. This is karmic action. What will be the experience when I truly practice the Noble Eightfold Path, the Nembutsu, sitting in Zazen, walking, chanting? To lose oneself and its limited views in such forms—these forms become emptiness. To lose oneself. Yes.

So, the question to you is, "Are you looking for something to happen?" You will have to answer that yourself.

That will be all of my dharma talk. Thank you.

"Who are you to say that This is not 'The Way'?"

> *We use judgments, morals, and societal values to figure out right and wrong. Is "The Way" bound to this right and wrong? Is the path to enlightenment bound to this right and wrong? Or, is it free of these concepts? Does it instead let all enter, including even those who are not "on the path"... the ones we say are a far cry from being there?*

A man walks as if he is going somewhere. But, he is constantly arriving here. Could this be called "The Way"? No matter what his thoughts or beliefs, he walks as if he is going somewhere. But, every time he arrives here.

Is "The Way" beyond comprehension? And, who is to say that This is not it? There is the person that is ignorant of it. There is the person that is aware of it. There it the person who does not care about it. Yet and still, they all walk and arrive here.

We are here at the Cleveland Buddhist Temple. We use a lot of words, trying to describe something. Is this "The Way"? We sit. We chant. We walk around the room. We may even say we are "aware" of it. Some may have what they call "experiences"—enlightenment experiences. Some may not have these experiences. Some may be totally ignorant of it. They may be here for a totally different quest. Is this "The Way"? Is it beyond understanding; beyond the limited words?

The Buddha had a number of experiences—as a prince, as a hermit, sitting, etc. He had many disappointments and many teachers. He went to one teacher and surpassed him and went to another because he found he could not awaken that way. Then we say that must have been the wrong path. But, was he not walking and arriving here?

There is a saying that we are standing in water up to our necks yet dying of thirst. We use judgments, morals, and societal values to figure out right and wrong. Is "The Way" bound to this right and wrong? Is the path to enlightenment bound to this right and wrong? Or, is it free of these concepts? Does it instead let all enter, including even those who are not "on the path" in terms of their belief or from the perspective of right and wrong, ethics, or societal values—the ones we say are a far cry from being there?

So, what are we learning about our experience and these others that we are interdependent with? Maybe we think we are advanced human beings, since we sit in a hot temple and practice Buddhism with a lot of intellectual knowledge about it. Perhaps we say that we will go out and teach others who are not on the right path. Why do we believe that they are not on the right path? Because it does not line up with our intellectual values, with our path. Yet, all karmic paths are here—interdependent and sitting in "The Way". From the birds, to the cars, to the accidents, to everything we believe is not there, and everything we believe that is there, and everything that is beyond our conceptual ideas and beliefs.

So, here we are--sitting here. And others, wherever they are—the seen and the unseen—are arriving here, beyond the aggregates of perception. They are arriving here. Even if it looks as if they are going somewhere, they are still arriving here.

We will use a term called "yesterday," which doesn't exist. Yesterday, I came here and there were six new people here. And each one of them believed that this was it. So, were they in ignorance? Or, did they arrive here? Are they going anywhere? Or, did they arrive here? Were others here for their arrival—others beyond perception, beyond seen and unseen? We walk right in that door. We arrive right here. There is not one seen thing leading us, but still we arrive right here—with absolutely no knowledge of where we are arriving. We can watch a small child walk right in here with no knowledge of where they are and we say they are not learning yet—they don't understand. But they arrive right here. "The Way" is shown, but still the intellect does not see because of beliefs, morals, ethics, and societal values. Yet it arrives right here, beyond understanding.

So, who is to say that whatever we see in belief—in the five skandhas and with the feelings—is not "The Way"? From drunken bums, to murderers, to thieves—who is to say that this is not "The Way", arriving right here? So, we may use limited viewpoints such as morals and right and wrong. But, who is to say that this is not "The Way"?

There are a lot of Zen stories about someone who stole everything but left the moon. Stories about ones that went to jail and came out to become a monk. We watch movies where thieves or murderers go through experiences that allow them to take over the Master's Way. These are "The Way".

That will be all of my dharma talk. Thank you.

"What you are seeking is empty."

> *We chant the words: "Form is sunyata. Sunyata is form." Yet, we are still here looking for something.... [W]e sit in search of enlightenment, a little peace, some understanding.... We are going to make a "better life." But it says right here that it is all empty.... Then we look in books to verify our existence or what we are doing here. It must make sense, to come to a temple and sit in the humidity, walk, chant, and sweat. So, we look for words to justify what we are doing—that it makes sense. Eliminate the words and how much sense does it make? So, we sit here and we are sitting beyond anything that makes sense. ... [W]hat we are sitting in is a mystery that doesn't make sense. That mystery is our lives.*

I find myself short of breath, because of the humidity, and with no inhaler. One could say: "This shouldn't be this way." But that statement would not make any sense because this is the way it is.

Years ago, when I first came here, Sensei Ogui would shut the doors at 7:00 p.m. for advanced meditation. Then the students would be outside banging on the door trying to get in. But the doors would be locked.

So, here we are at the Cleveland Buddhist Temple, looking for something. We chant the words: "Form is sunyata. Sunyata is form." Yet, we are still here looking for something. The words that we use in our search are empty. The form is empty. Emptiness is sunyata.

So, here we are looking for something while at the very same time we chant words that tell us that what we are looking for is empty. There is nothing to get out of it. Still, we sit in search of enlightenment, a little peace, some understanding—a lot words. We are going to make a "better life." But it says right here that it is all empty.

We chant a lot things while we are sitting here—and the words contradict what we are doing. Or, we contradict what the words are saying. Then we look in books to verify our existence or what we are doing here. It must make sense, to come to a temple and sit in the humidity, walk, chant, and sweat. So, we look for words to justify what we are doing—

that it makes sense. Eliminate the words and how much sense does it make? Eliminate "enlightenment", eliminate the word "Buddha", eliminate the word "Zazen" and everything else and how much sense does it make? Eliminate trying to find the "truth"—that is empty anyway. Eliminate these words and ask yourself how much sense what we are doing here makes.

So, we sit here and we are sitting beyond anything that makes sense. Koans are expressed here, along with a number of other tools that say that what we are sitting in is a mystery that doesn't make sense. That mystery is our lives.

I have this life that does not act naturally. Do you know why? Because before I take any action I think about it. I apply morals, ethics, and societal values. So, I have a plan. If I came to the door there, I would look in and see what was going on and try and find the easiest way to get in without disturbing anyone. I like the way little kids do this. They look in, see everyone sitting down, then they jump right in without any plan at all—jumping over chairs till they get to their seat.

Boom! There it is. No plan. They engage in life while I engage in morals and ethics and societal values.

So, when I leave here I will have a plan. When I go to the store I have a plan as to what I am going to get, etc. Everything will be already formed in my preconceived ideas about what the right amount of money should be and where everything should be. But when I get there something may be out. Dang! Then, something else may have gone up in price. God forbid! But that may happen. Then, there it is: suffering—created in my plans.

So, I do not act quite naturally. In my plans I know how much I am going to spend and how much I need to last me into the future. I wish the dog and the cat could understand this and save their food. But they eat it all up right there. They do not worry about this "future". Kids don't either. So, in my plan I create suffering.

Yet and still, I read sutras and say I have faith in the Buddha, or the dharma, or the sangha. But yet I still have my plan. There it is. Sits right there. So, do I arrive with Amidha Buddha, infinite wisdom and boundless compassion?

Another saying states that if we stay close to the dharma—in it we will be provided with everything we need. No future, no past, but in this breath everything that is necessary is supplied. I have not gotten to that point, but I have experienced it. Yes. Things appear at the exact precise moment they are needed—right there. Not before, not after, not at the "wrong" time—but exactly in that breath. Exactly what is needed.

So, am I really studying this dharma? Or, am I using beliefs, preconceived ideas, plans, formations—that are empty?

So, here I am—sitting, walking, chanting. Do I have a plan? Do I have preconceived ideas? Am I looking for something? Thus we are told: When you sit, just sit; When you walk, just walk; When you chant, just chant. Am I looking for a better chant? A better sit? A walk that will amaze me? What am I looking for?

So, here I am. Sitting in the dharma with ignorance. Not realizing the two that are here. Not harmonizing them and going through. These plans, sunyata, emptiness, form, words—not harmonizing them and going through.

My teacher often said: "Craig, when you walk in the forest and there is dew all over the place and you have just started out—just keep going. Don't stop. Just keep going and become a part of it all. And before you know it you will be amazed. There will be dew all over you. Just keep walking." He would also take things from books like: "If you see the Buddha on the road, kill him."

Just keep walking.

He also focused on the word "conclusion." A person would read a book and in the end there would be a conclusion to that book. Sensei would say there is no conclusion. Just keep walking. Go beyond your plan. Look just to the things that are around.

I have also said: "Since you are here, why not?" Some of you have heard me say that in the beginner's class. Since you are here, sitting and walking—why not? Just walk. The plans are going to come back in. You can invite them in and then let them go. Then just sit and walk. When you leave you can pick your plans back up and take them wherever you go. But while you are here—why not?

Sensei would also often ask: "Who brought you here?" We would come up with all sorts of words for who brought us here. The newer people would say: "My friend brought me."

Then he would ask: "Do you have the switch turned on, so you can receive?" Is the switch turned on? And, who brought you here?

So, if you are here—why not? Let go of the plan. Just walk. Just chant. Just sit.

And that will be all of my dharma talk. Thank you.

"You are an infinite possibility."

> *That is what we are looking for—infinite possibilities. This is said to relieve or stop suffering. . . . [T]here is no need to look for infinite possibility. You are it!*

Things change. The trees that used to be in front of the Temple have been removed, and now something else will start to grow. Conditions change. We sit here in these conditions—we sit, walk, and chant in these conditions. We chant the Nembutsu—infinite light and boundless life. Sitting and chanting the Nembutsu, we sit in possibilities—infinite possibilities. That is what we are looking for—infinite possibilities. This is said to relieve or stop suffering.

Find emptiness. In emptiness there are possibilities. Shunryu Suzuki talks about possibilities—infinite possibilities. He also talks about a mind that is full of speculation and the idea that there are very few possibilities. Sometimes I may wonder what possibilities we are looking for. Are we looking for a miracle? Maybe we are looking for the possibility of enlightenment, Satori, or different words like that. We talk about standing in water up to our necks and dying of thirst. Chant the Nembutsu: Namu Amida Butsu. Infinite light and boundless compassion. Yes.

So, does one that sits there realize that his life is the only life that is sitting there? In the whole vast universe, his life is the only life sitting there? Does he realize that with billions of people on earth, his is the only life that he is experiencing right here? Does he realize that out of lives as vast as the grains of sand on the earth—insects, animals, whatever—his is the only life that he is experiencing? But yet and still, we ask: "What is this infinite possibility?" Not knowing that our life is that possibility—that mystery that sits right there out of trillions of things. That was the possibility—that you were born into human form and arrived right here.

So, there is no need to look for infinite possibility. You are it!

Once you move away from the rationalizing mind, the suffering mind, you realize that out of all the stars above and everything else around, no one else has your life. How did such a thing happen? We know about the laws of cause and effect, but how did such a thing happen—this infinite possibility? The words that I use boomerang around and say: "You are the possibility." How did this happen right here?

Hard is it to be born into human life, yet now we are living it. Difficult is it to hear the teachings of the Blessed One or the dharma, yet now we hear it. Here we are, freeing ourselves from the oceans of birth and death—being one of these possibilities, and on a karmic path. We are on this karmic path because of others—all the other possibilities.

We are looking for possibilities out there in what we call the transitory and impermanent world. Things are constantly changing. This includes our own life, which is also changing in the same way. But we do not consider ourselves as the possibility. Rather, we see ourselves as the viewer of it. We identify with the suffering limited mind, instead of seeing ourselves as the infinite possibility.

We talk about oneness and use words such as "interdependence." But when it really comes down to it, we ask: "How did this happen?" Can I grasp that I am the only one that is living this life? No one is living this life except for me. My life is existing right here, and all of This makes it possible—this possibility, right here.

And I think that will be all of my dharma talk. Thank you.

"When will This be enough?"

> *Look at the dharma—the rain that you walk in. Look beyond your beliefs. Your beliefs will never manifest anyway because This is here, not your belief. See This, and then you will have arrived into infinite wisdom and boundless compassion. . . . See This and you will know that you have arrived into something that not one word in the human language can describe—not one word.*

One may say: "I am grateful for such kindness that allows your life to be so situated that it is here and nowhere else in the universe."

There is a saying Reverend Ogui used to be fond of repeating: "No matter what you believe, when you walk in the rain you will get wet." No matter where you wish to be, your life is here. Whatever delusional other time you think would be best for you, your life is here.

When you take a breath sitting here, that breath is beyond everything. It is the only breath. It is sufficient and enough in itself—right here. But yet and still, as human beings we always want more. We always thirst after more. We always look for "better". And we try to pull happiness out of things that are on their own karmic path that has no "happiness" in it for us to pull out—there is only its karmic path.

So, when will this breath be enough—arriving right here? This breath of infinite wisdom and boundless compassion, life itself, when will I recognize it and be grateful that it is here? These conditions have never existed anywhere else in the universe. I arrive into them for the very first time. When will that be enough?

There once was a group of people that came here that was looking for something. They were looking for degrees, position, prestige, jobs. They were going to college and doing a lot of different things and they were having troubles. That is what they called it, "troubles." We could call it ignorance. Basically, they were complaining that things were not going the way their plans said they should go. They went to lower laws such as morals, ethics, societal values, and they could not get their thirst satisfied.

So, I told them: "All you have to do is look." Look at the dharma—the rain that you walk in. Look beyond your beliefs. Your beliefs will never manifest anyway because This is here, not your belief. See This, and then you will have arrived into infinite wisdom and boundless compassion. Beyond limited viewpoints. Beyond "more." Beyond degrees. Beyond prestige. See This and you will know that you have arrived into something that not one word in the human language can describe—not one word.

There were two young ladies here earlier and I asked one of them her name. And she said "Abby" or "Becky" or something like that. And I asked her when she got that name. And she said she got it when she was born. And I asked her who gave her that name. And she said her parents gave her that name. And I asked her: "What was your name before that? What were you before that name?" And she said before that she was a baby. And then I asked her what she was before she was born. What was your face before you were born?

The word "born" is a word you learned here. What were you before that happened? Before that word limited you to a "baby"? Something crawls by and we call it a baby. Then we've got to separate the babies, so we'll call that one Becky. What were you before that? No word can explain that.

But yet and still we look at form as if it is going to bring us something. As if all we have to do is get enough of this form together and then we will be happy. We seek to control more of this form.

I once talked about dichotomy and dualism. How you see form: You see the seen, but you do not see the unseen. I talked about why it is there. I talked about infinite possibilities, boundless compassion, things that are coming into sight, and those that are going out of sight. Beyond these two that are moving, one might say there is "emptiness."

Yes, things are constantly changing, arriving here in this breath. And they have never existed before. So, is that enough? Can we examine our lives in the here and now? Can we depend on the Buddha or the enlightened ones? Can we depend on what we chant? If so, we might arrive here and no where else.

So many sacrifices. How many things do you think have changed that are unseen that make our life possible? That car that just went by, in this breath—that one right there. Did you see it? How many things make our life possible? Do we live in the compassion and kindness of others?

Someone might come here when the temple is empty and ask: "Where is everybody at?" They are right here. That is what makes this life right here possible, because they are here. The unseen: The statues, candles, incense, cushions, sabutons, safus, the chairs…the unseen. Or, did these things just appear by themselves? The unseen are here.

Where do we live? Do we live separate, or are we interdependent with everything?

What is my life? Does it just stop at my skin, at what I can see? Or, is it the universe?

So, when will I wake up beyond ignorance? In ignorance I am trapped between good and bad, right and wrong, like and dislike. When will I wake up beyond this ignorance and say: "In this breath I arrived here, and this is my life—beyond any comparison"? And in this life everything is a mystery and unique. In the blink of an eye, it has already changed. Boom! Yes, this is my life.

So, one listens to the gong—the ringing of it. They hear the bells of the church. They stop and listen. It says: "This is your life—pay attention to it right here." This is the sound of the gong. To listen to this—to stop—that is enlightenment. Or, one may say: "To wake up one must realize that my life exists nowhere except here." And this life, or this breath, is enough.

And I think that will be all of my dharma talk. Thank you.

"There is no 'more' in This."

> *In the here and now I am looking for a "better" that cannot exist in the here and now. The trees cannot be "better", the arrangements here cannot be "better", the elusiveness of the incense that shows how your life is cannot be "better". This exact moment and the breath that you take cannot be "better". But yet and still we want more. But it cannot give more. Not one thing here can give "more".*

Even in the heat, the humidity, and the chirping crickets, one may say: "I am grateful to have come here and sat." Bringing ignorance here, to sit with it. Even bringing the thirst of wanting something different—bringing that here, too.

A guy named Tim McCarthy says that if you were to eat a Lay's potato chip, you could not eat just one. Always, there is another one. He also says that life is not satisfying. Call it suffering, or whatever. There is always the delusion of wanting more. Always the fears that are there—of old age, death, or losing something that I think I have. Always this thirst that hinders me from entering into life itself.

The things that arrive here have no worry or concern for these things. These things are a taught process from a society—its morals and ethics. Born into This, the five aggregates awaken in forms, and separation, and perceptions, and what is stored in consciousness as memory. Memorizing a "better" time or a "good" time, and wanting more of it. Believing that in life itself there must be more than what we have here. And believing that I am running out of time to get it. Thus, I trample on life itself looking for something that does not even exist. Yes, I am looking for something that does not even exist.

In the here and now I am looking for a "better" that cannot exist in the here and now. The trees cannot be "better", the arrangements here cannot be "better", the elusiveness of the incense that shows how your life is cannot be "better". This exact moment and the breath that you take cannot be "better". But yet and still we want more. But it cannot give more. Not one thing here can give "more". And in every moment that it arrives—it cannot give any more than what it is. It cannot be better than what it is. And it is also on a karmic path. Using another tradition, one may say that these things arise out of God himself. They are not here for man to value. They are just here, moving on their karmic path.

The mind of ignorance has always disturbed such things. Yes, separated it and placed a value on it. Added words like "beautiful" and called it a "flower" and a "rose" and come to conclusions like: "it is worth a dollar". Or called it a "weed" and a "dandelion" and concluded that "it should be destroyed". This we do with everything. So, the suffering is created out of ignorance.

Everything is on its karmic path. And the things that we believe will make us happy do not. They are empty. They are moving on this path. They have no "value" in a sense. They are life itself. So, there is no "better"— that belief is delusional. There is no "more"—it is delusional to think there is. There is no "happiness" that can be taken out of this—it is delusional to seek for such a thing.

Our life exists right here because these things are on their karmic path. We are living in the kindness of other things that our ignorance has altered, and our minds have altered, from their true self or true nature. And if ignorant mind has done that to the life itself that you see out here moving around—what has it done to what came here?

There was something that came here. I always like to call it "the Other". It had not title. It was never late (a kid told me that once). It had no where to go. It was here. It was free from the delusion of a self. And it responded naturally before it became conscious of "Craig" and societal values and time. Yes, it was just here.

One says that when a person chants the words "Namu Amida Butsu" it is not you that is chanting—it is the Nembutsu or the Buddha that is calling you. Yes. Others use words such as "God" and different things, and they say things, but it is not them that is saying it—it is It calling them.

So, I ask people: "Who brought you here to the Temple? Who brought this ignorant one here? Whatever your name is, who brought it here? What called it to the Cleveland Buddhist Temple? And, what are you looking for?" So, you would look. And all this stuff is here and you would look at it and there is nothing here but yet and still you want something out of it. Something "more" than what it is.

I say: "Take a breath." And they would take it and I would ask: "Is that enough, right there, that one breath?" Do you know that in that one breath was infinite wisdom and boundless compassion? The entire universe supported that one breath. Is that enough? The whole universe—since you are interdependent with all of these things—supported that one breath. But the limited mind is looking for another Lay's potato chip—looking for more. Yes.

So, here we are, sitting at the Cleveland Buddhist Temple. Cars are passing, crickets are making noise outside, and we are just sitting, just walking, just chanting, with the incense, fire, humidity, and heat—we are sitting in it. And one may say, that for all of this infinite wisdom and boundless compassion, my life is the only life here experiencing this. I am here because of the seen and unseen, that which is coming and that which is leaving—at least in appearance. And because of all the things that make these things possible, one may sit here in the heat and be uncomfortable and say: "I am grateful."

And that will be all of my dharma talk. Thank you.

"Lose yourself in this breath."

> *I asked the people yesterday whether [their one breath] was enough and not one of them said yes. Not one could even find gratitude for having received the breath because there was something more that they wanted. So, where are we to find the freedom from suffering? In the next breath? In "more"? Or, is it in this one?*

Gassho—a sign of respect. At the Cleveland Buddhist Temple, we say your life is respected here without wanting it to change. Whether you are a "good" person or a "bad" person or indifferent, your life is respected. It is the only life it can be, existing in the here and now. It can be no different.

Yet and still, I have trouble with that life. Belief has always said it should be different. I depend on that life, and the lives of others, to make my life meaningful and happy. Or, we may say "satisfying." But yet and still, I keep thirsting after other things. If things would only be just a little different, if we could only do a few different things, then everything would be all right. Yes.

Things are constantly changing. The leaves will be falling soon—they are changing colors. Everything that appears in the here and now, right now, is exactly as it is—the dharma. So, when will I use infinite wisdom and boundless compassion to see that life? Instead of adding morals, ethics, societal teachings, beliefs, and everything else that I have been taught—preconceived ideas viewing that life. When will I see it from an infinite position? That whatever is taking place is happening in the here and now, and it can be none other than what it is. You cannot change it. It is on a karmic path you cannot change. When will I realize that it being on this karmic path makes my life full? The word "full" is still empty, but we shall use "full." So, as long as it is on its karmic path and I use infinite wisdom and boundless compassion, then my life is as it is.

I once asked someone about "enough"—I talked about this in the last class. I asked them to take a breath. And they took a breath and I asked them whether that was enough. And

I went down the line and not one person said that was enough. So, going down the line—take a breath. Is that enough?

Student #1: "Nope."

Go on. Take a breath. Is that enough?

Student #2: "It's good."

It's good. Take a breath. Is that enough?

Student #3: "What else is there?"

Go on. Is that enough?

Student #4: "Certainly seems to be enough for this moment?"

Take a breath. What do you have to say? Is that enough?

Student #5: "No. I'm hungry too." [*Laughter.*]

Take a breath. Is that enough?

Student #6: "For now."

For now. So, tell me, if it is enough for now—is there any other? We have just talked about infinite wisdom and boundless compassion. We have also talked about the fact that we are interdependent with all things—the whole universe is us. There are things moving into existence and out of existence. There are infinite and boundless things happening. There are things that are passing away and things that are being born, the seen and the unseen—all in that one breath. It took all of those things doing exactly what they did to make this moment. And you want them to do more? If you believe This isn't enough, then they have to do more.

That one breath and all of those things—infinite possibilities—have taken place. And yet you want more. When will This be enough? The universe in one breath.

Ignorance comes because we use memory and we are always looking for the next one of something we previously experienced as pleasurable—we are always thirsting after something—instead of arriving in that one breath. Ignorance is the belief that the next breath is basically the same as the last breath. Just like the person who walks down the stairs and breathes. When he arrives here, he is not the same person he was when he was walking down the stairs. At the time he took the first breath he did not even know what was going to happen. Time has passed. Now, this breath is the only breath.

It is not measured by the "more" of what he wanted, or something "more" desired in the future—there is no such thing. This breath is the only one that exists.

So, I asked the people yesterday whether it was enough and not one of them said yes. Not one could even find gratitude for having received the breath because there was something more that they wanted. So, where are we to find the freedom from suffering? In the next breath? In "more"? Or, is it in this one?

In the dharma they say: "Hard is it to be born into human life, now we are living it. Difficult is it to hear the teachings of the Blessed One, now we hear them. If we do not deliver ourselves from the ocean of birth and death, there is no other time that we can." Yes. So, you do not have to worry about becoming enlightened or waking up in the future.

Shunryu Suzuki talked about ordinary mind and nothing special. Yes. Infinite possibilities happening in nothing special—this breath. What do you believe enlightenment or awareness is? Something where we float on clouds or incense? Or, is it the natural state of man—what they talk about in most Zen books, that man has lost his true nature? In other words, he does not simply respond to life. Instead, he always plans and brings in preconceived ideas about how everything should go. Then nothing seems to go right and life does not seem to treat him well. This is because he seems to be separated from his life. So, when will we lose our self in this breath? When will this one be enough?

In the Tuesday beginners' sittings I tell them that they will only be sitting for 12 minutes, since they are wiggling a lot. [*Laughter.*] So, I tell them not to think about time and when the gong is going to ring. Lose yourself in this breath right here. Twelve minutes can only pass in one breath. The gong will ring in one breath. That's right. The breathing does not lie in time. It is beyond time. Walking meditation does not have anything to do with time—how many rounds, how many steps—it goes beyond. Breath counting has nothing to do with time. The "one," the "two," will all disappear. You will arrive beyond time and beyond numbers into infinite possibilities in the walking and the chanting and the sitting.

So, when will that one (and beyond that one) when will the infinite beyond that one breath be enough? When will we use these forms to go through and enter into that one—waking up from the ocean of birth and death? Yes.

And that will be all of my dharma talk. Thank you.

"There is actually nothing to do."

> *What do you want? You are sitting right here—what do you want? If it exists, you should be able to get it. If you do not have it, it must not exist. So, what do you want?*

What is your name?

Student: Debra.

Who were you before you were "Debra"?

It is a good question: Who was I before my name? Does Debra depend on Amida Buddha, infinite wisdom, or boundless compassion? Or, does Debra depend on what she learned after she became Debra? What she learned in terms of time, in terms of numbers, in terms of beliefs, in dichotomies of right and wrong. So, who do you depend on? Do we depend on limited objectives that we have learned to depend on? Or, do we depend on infinite wisdom and boundless compassion?

Let us just say that limited objectives may not be true. So, we will say they may cause what we will call suffering.

They do not come out the way we planned for them to come out, or the way we assume they should come out. So, they may cause suffering. Limited objectives seem to be tied to a thought that is derived from past experience—something that we learned and that may have words attached to it such as "good" and "bad", "right" and "wrong", and on and on.

So, in these conditions we may depend on these limited objectives and then things do not work out the way we want them to work out. So, we try some more. Yes, we have received the dharma, or the truth—we are sitting in it. But yet and still, we want more—and this causes suffering.

One may ask: When will we wake up to infinite possibilities? And one may respond: Well, what is that—infinite possibilities? So, I ask: Who were you before you were born? Yes. Who brought you here, in these conditions? There seems to be something at work. But yet and still, once we get here we try and figure out what we should do. We rely on past experiences instead of letting them go and arriving here. There is actually nothing to do. Not one thing.

So, here we are, coming in to the Cleveland Buddhist Temple and still causing suffering. Yes. We are depending on limited objectives: To sit well, to walk well, to chant well. Not realizing that these are forms that are empty. Yes, they are empty. But yet and still, we put our whole selves into this emptiness with the hope of getting something out of it. But they are empty. We do this even though when we come into the Cleveland Buddhist Temple, infinite wisdom and boundless compassion is already here.

Yesterday, I was talking to a young gentleman here. I told him that when he took a breath, the whole universe supported that one breath. Things were coming into existence (as we understand things through the use of words) and leaving out of existence—dying and being born—and everything in between. But he said he wanted more. The whole universe supported that one breath, but he wanted something more. He wanted his limited objective. Yes.

The "more" that he wanted was called an "A" for his class in the future that does not exist. And that "A" caused suffering in the here and now. He wanted that "A". So, when he gets that "A"—what will he want then? Something more.

So, I arrive into infinite possibilities—the whole universe supporting one breath—but that is not enough. This mystery of my interdependence with all things—I am breathing, so many functions are going on right now that I am not controlling. But yet and still, my life is right here. Food is provided, house is provided, friends are provided, everything is provided—and I am not in control of any of them. But the delusion of "more" or the "A"—I would like to be in control of that which causes suffering. All to say that I exist because I have an "A" to prove it. Instead of Buddha, or the One that came before my name, that has no title and needs no "A". Yes.

So, here I am. Born into human life. Yes—it is very hard to be born into human life. Also, there is so much literature and words talking about something that does not exist. Have you ever read any of that stuff? They talk about Nirvana, they talk about Buddha Nature, they talk about Heaven and God and Hell, they talk about all these different things that do not even exist while I am sitting right here. We read about them.

So, here we are sitting at the Cleveland Buddhist Temple having heard about all these different things that are basically trying to describe a mystery. It almost sounds like a fairy tale. And yet people believe in these things enough to kill in the name of them. But it sounds almost like a fairy tale. It is almost as if I am thirsting for something, and I think it is an "A". That is what I think I am thirsting for. And this is called ignorance. I believe it is an "A" or some other object I have learned of here. But what if what I am really thirsting for is from the unnamed that did not need an "A" or any of my limited objectives? That which they say moves in and out of my senses. What if it is actually right here moving in and out of my sense and that is what I am searching for?

Lots of people have seen the 10 ox-herding pictures. You are looking for something. You are not even sure what it is. Then you see some footprints and decide this must be what you are looking for. Then you see the hind part of the bull.

Then you see the whole bull. Then you get on the bull. You are still searching. Then the bull and you disappear. But the whole point of it is—is not the bull you? That is going to the Source, realizing it, then coming back. And it talks about coming back in rags, but full. Things are not what they appear to be, nor are they otherwise.

There is a story about a great Zen master who was invited to a banquet in his honor. And kings and queens were there in their finest dress. And he arrived dressed in rags and he sat down, and even though he was the guest of honor everyone ignored him. So, he started to feed his clothes. And he said something about the appearance of things.

So, they are searching for something. In all the books, they are searching for something. They think it is Nirvana or Enlightenment. They are looking for this word and they believe that it has something more than the delusion that it is written for. They think it has something. They are looking for Heaven. They want an experience with God. But yet and still they are carried by infinite possibilities and can not even explain or control the function of this body. Basically, they are what one would call asleep at the helm. Yes, something else is running it and they are asleep at the helm.

So, one may ask: Are we looking for what is moving in and out of our senses—that which has always been there and has no title? Yes. Heart beats, lungs take in air. Every time we appear—just like that candle that changes constantly and so fast—every time we appear, the whole universe is there and supports that. Including disappearing and becoming and beyond. The whole universe supports that. So, you don't have to worry about death. Don't even save any money for it. It is not true that you need $5000 to die. It does not cost anything to die. You do not need to worry about dying. And there are a lot of other myths that just are not true and you do not have to worry about them. So, all you have to do is take your breath. We will say that there is a thing that is moving in and out of your senses that is at the helm. And what you are looking for is already there. It is not in anything else. Everything else is empty, just like you.

Moving towards the One that has no title, you may even forget your name. Have you ever heard stories of Zen masters that have forgotten their name—moving closer to the One that has no title. The one that has no title does not need enlightenment— only the delusion does. The belief of a self needs Enlightenment or Heaven. This self creates some weird things. It created a Heaven with Angels and put it in the clouds. And guess what, when it gets there it will remain young forever and all its people will be there. All its limited objects—brothers, sisters, all of them will be there and we will have a great time in Heaven. I will invent a God to take care of all that for me. Yes.

But your life is right here. The mystery is: How did you get here? And why are these conditions like this? What are these things—these people—out here? Am I interested in them? I am the only one that is experiencing this life as if there was something out there. I am the only one having this experience. Interdependent with this reflection that is reflecting everything back. When will I go through it? When will I understand that this is my life—nothing other? And the "A" does not exist in it. It is not there. This is my life. The reason the "A" does not exist is because all this is here, and this life is supported by the whole universe.

So, a person may ask: "So where does the 'A' come in?" If you never worried about the "A" and moved closer to the dharma, someone may grade your paper and give you an "A" but you would not even notice or care. And, what they gave you would automatically have gratitude in it. Because, as you move closer to it, you are always grateful. In every condition, whatever is received—from right to wrong to bad or whatever—whatever is received—from ignorance to everything else—I am grateful, that such wisdom has made my life as it is. No matter whether it is "right" or "wrong", I have received. No matter whether you get cursed or not.

Zen masters can be very strange. They go beyond the monasteries. The monastery is at the foot of the hill and they go to the top and just hang out. Yes, they are very, very strange. But, they have received.

So, here we are at the Cleveland Buddhist Temple, looking for a name. When will you realize—Reverend Ogui used to say—when will you realize that every other thing has given enough? This is it, right here. This is your life.

So, here we are. What will you do? What is there to do? Where is there to go? Look at it. I am like my father and he has already passed. And others also. I was watching a movie with Kinsley and they said: "It is shocking to grow old." But is not that a societal value. What is that?

What do you want? What do you want? You are sitting right here—what do you want? If it exists, you should be able to get it. If you do not have it, it must not exist. So, what do you want?

So, here we are—still thirsting for the next potato chip. But, we are here. Wisdom and compassion are here. They are the One that moves in and out of our senses. They are sending little signals out trying to wake up the ignorance of "Craig" and "Debra" and "You". They send little signals out in the form of things not going your way. Waiting to wake up ignorance because they want to join with it. They are the thing that says that if I do not wake up and stop suffering here and now in this ocean of birth and death, there is no other time. Just sending little signals out.

Don't you feel like there is something there? There has to be something there for us to go to funny looking churches and listen to people. There has to be something there. What are they talking about? You go places—Zen places, Yoga places, to see the Dalia Lama—because there has to be something there. What is the reason? It is a sense of something. But it is a faint sense. You cannot even explain why you are going. "I hear so-and-so is coming." There is something there. What is it that attracts you there? Or, are you just going to be entertained? Don't you have a little sense of there being something there?

Now, more than likely it will not wake up at the event. It will wake up here—and I do not mean the Cleveland Buddhist Temple. It will wake up *here*.

And that will be all of my dharma talk. Thank you.

"Arriving in this breath—no suffering."

> *The ignorance of the mind, via the five aggregates and skandhas, the teachings of society and learned behaviors, has brought me to this idea that there is something more—something to prepare for, something that will make meaning to life. I am not aware that I am standing in it and have arrived into it, with nothing to do.*

Take a breath. Think about taking a breath. But the breath that is not thought about has no preconceived ideas, it has no suffering to it. Yes, but yet and still we still suffer. But it has no suffering. The dharma, as it truly is, has no suffering—it has simply a karmic path.

So, here we are, sitting here—sitting with the breath. It is effortless—it comes in, it leaves out. The candle that is burning is just about gone, yet it has no problem. It just a karmic path—no suffering. When the light is out, it is gone. The apples are just being apples—no suffering. No comparison, no limits, they simply are as they are. They are not wishing to be oranges or anything—or "better". They simply are as they are. There is no suffering.

We sit and prepare for a future. Who causes suffering? Who causes suffering? Sitting, preparing for a future. Indoctrinated into this life. Or, we might say, born into it. Things have become habitual. Doing the same things over and over. Preparing, studying, future, time—running out of it, old age, death. All of these things, moving toward a future that does not exist. But the breath—effortless—has no suffering.

So, I asked a person here once: "You are sitting right here. What do you have to do?" And once they came up with the words of what they had to do, it never took place. It is something that they never had and never took place—it had the labels of suffering. But the breath was arriving here. Their life arriving right here. Nothing to do. Everything in the universe that is interdependent arrived right here with that breath. Enough. No suffering. Karmic path. Everything else did not come here, arrive here, comparing itself with something else. There is nothing else. Everything is interdependent, doing exactly what it is.

The ignorance of the mind, via the five aggregates and skandhas, the teachings of society and learned behaviors, has brought me to this idea that there is something more—something to prepare for, something that will make meaning to life. I am not aware that I am standing in it and have arrived into it, with nothing to do.

So, what does the breath do when it arrives here—since that is your life? What does the breath do when you arrive here—since that is your life? The heart beats, the mind arrives, everything is here. Yes, everything is here. What ignorance is it that makes me think that there should be something different? That things should go a certain way?

The leaves will fall exactly where they fall, and I will say they need to be somewhere else. The arrangement of things—of a form. Yes. Apples will fall out of a tree.

In some instance, a person will try to compare his life with others—things that are arriving. Not realizing that his life is those others. If he came here not struggling he would watch things and there would be nothing for him to do. Yes. But if he looks and compares he might say: "I want to trade places." But his life is so situated, so unique, that it is right here with nothing to do. Everything is moving, but he does not find this interesting. He has to do something. Yes. Present himself in a certain way. Use morals and ethics in his life.

Zen masters once sat around, had a few words, and then said: "Enough is enough. Let us have a cup of tea." Really, there is nothing to do. So why not enjoy the tea? Trees, the garden, everything doing what it does—they have all provided for me to sit here and have a cup of tea. So, someone may look around here using perception and ask: "Where is everyone at? Where is everybody?" But they are why you are here. They are on their karmic path. Are you enjoying your life? Are you kind, using wisdom and compassion?

So, here we are. Sitting, walking, chanting. Are we trying to be better? Or, are we arriving in the step, the breath, the inhalation? Did we arrive in the inhalation? Did you arrive in the exhalation? Did we go between both of them and beyond? Did we arrive in the seen? Did we arrive in the unseen? Interdependent, sitting here, walking, what was there to do? Yes. Where was the suffering? Was the suffering in the mind when it said: "Time is too long. Time is too short." Was it born of the body, mouth, thought—in time, right here, was it born? Does zazen sit outside of time? Or, are we sitting in time? Does zazen sit outside of time? Time has no bearing on zazen. In ken-hin, do we walk twice around? Do we walk for fifteen minutes? Do we think about the time?

Ken-hin cannot be done in time. Zazen cannot be done in time. These are beyond time. This can only be done now. In the here and now. No other place. So, if you are looking toward tomorrow to do zazen or ken-hin you can forget it. You have already created suffering. If you are looking forward to an hour from now, or when you get home, you have already created suffering. So, from zazen to ken-hin to awareness practice right here.

Once I asked: "Did you enjoy your sit?" And they said: "Yes, we really enjoyed it." Then I said: "Then why do you leave?" Because all of them had somewhere to go and something to do. And they could not figure it out. Because of the separation and going somewhere but not arriving into each breath or each step or the awareness practice of zen meditation. Arriving into it every moment. Into zazen, in all practice, into ken-hin—moving.

So, once they realized they said: "Yes!" Right here sitting, in the car sitting, in the house sitting, at the job sitting, walking, ken-hin. Arriving every moment. Never leaving. Yes.

A teacher once said, awareness practice—awake practice—is the hardest of all of the meditations. There are so many distractions out here. In Jodo Shin Soo, it is taking Amida Buddha into all your affairs—saying: "Namu Amida Butsu. Namu Amida Butsu. Namu Amida Butsu." The hardest practice is at your jobs, in your activities, at the barbecue, in everything else. That is the hardest practice. One is so distracted by the names of things around him, including amusement parks and everything else. So distracted, that we are easily uprooted from our true nature.

So, here we are. Right here. Arriving in this breath. Aware that this breath has no suffering. If I could arrive in this breath, there would be no suffering. As soon as I leave it, what happens? I have to do this, I have to take care of that, I need this, I am late for that, I am supposed to be somewhere, or whatever. But arriving in this breath—no suffering.

And that will be all of my dharma talk. Thank you.

"There is nothing 'short' or 'long' about a life—there is just life itself."

> *[H]e awakened her to the dharma—to the way things really are.*

Impermanence.

Ten days ago, Reverand Siebuhr was here from the Chicago Buddhist Temple. I was downstairs, former presidents of the Cleveland Buddhist Temple were there, and the woman who put together Sensei Ogui's book "Zen Shin Talks"—Mary Gove—was there with her husband, Dennis, who she met here. And we talked about old times, had cookies and tea—Reverend Siebuhr and a few of us. That was two Sundays ago. Monday they called, and Dennis was dead.

So, impermanence.

He had said he was feeling much better.

It makes me wonder, how did one enjoy their life? And what was the influence and impact of that life? Reverend Ogui used to come up here after a person had passed away and ask: "Did you enjoy your life?" And he would also say something about the importance of things. What was important? Your life, or the things that were in your life? You are not taking anything with you. But did you enjoy your life?

So, here we are. Ten days later the call comes in and the word goes out. The funeral is planned, the memorial service—everything is planned. What can one say to one that has lost a loved one? As if there are words that could explain such an event. Perhaps only the word: "impermanence."

There is a story about a woman that lost her baby and was told that the Buddha had great power. So, she took her dead baby to the Buddha and asked him to bring her baby back to life. He told her he could do that if she could get a mustard seed from the house where no one inside had lost a loved one or family member. So she went about from house to house, but she could not find any house that was free from such loss. Then she was awakened and buried her baby. It is also said that she then became one of his disciples. He did not say what he could not do or anything else. But he awakened her to the dharma—to the way things really are.

The baby took a breath—though we would say not very many (because of perception)—and then passed. But the last breath, whether it is in a baby or full-grown adult, is the same. It is the last breath. So, there is nothing "short" or "long" about a life. There is just life itself—that breath.

So, Dennis and I—or what appeared to be Dennis and I—were having a cup of tea, and eating cookies, and laughing about how wonderful his health was. Nothing else happened.

Yes, how are we enjoying our lives? Since impermanence and, some would say, unpredictability mean that things are constantly changing. There will be people that have not seen one another in (using linear time) many years. And they will come to the Temple—all the ones that sat here before. But they will not be the people that sat here before. They will all look different. Yes. Because conditions are never recurring. Yet the kindness of someone else makes it happen.

So, one can say that we live in the sacrifice of others. We live in the kindness of their misfortune, if that is a word that we can use, to bring such events as are necessary.

I had no reason to go across town—I had no reason to come here—this weekend. Unless an event happened that made it possible. (Hypothetically speaking, because I have not made it there yet.) It is kindness to bring people that I have drank tea with and ate cookies with together.

People may look at it and see karmic paths and conditions all around me making things possible. Going beyond the "right" and "wrong" and "good" and "bad" and suffering and everything. Going beyond this—is it not amazing? Yes, is it not amazing? Just ten days ago, we were smiling and having cookies. Just ten days ago. Is it not amazing how things, or conditions, bring other things together. And then apart. Together. And then apart.

So, here we are, at the Cleveland Buddhist Temple. And we can say that the sacrifice of others—someone has passed somewhere—has brought this event right here to allow us to sit together. The words to explain such an event are just as lacking as the words to explain the loss of a loved one to Mary Gove. So too, there are "no words" here to explain this.

So, in one of the Zen books it talks about walking on the bones of others. So, here we are at the Cleveland Buddhist Temple, beyond that but here. Appearing here on our karmic path. In the great sacrifice of others. Some could go past that word "sacrifice" and just rest in the impermanence of these conditions—transient and moving here.

So, here we are. Moving on. Constantly changing and becoming. Literally birth and death at the same time— breathing in and breathing out. Others make us aware of our lives. Going beyond regret and what I should have done. Things make me aware of my life. To pay attention to it and others right now because it is so impermanent and constantly changing. Just like the incense and the candle that just burned out. So impermanent. [*To student:*] Your incense stopped midway, didn't it? [*Laughter.*] Boom—not burning anymore. That's it.

So, here we are. Sensei would ask: "Are you enjoying your life?" He would also say: "You are not taking anything with you. So, are you enjoying your life?" He would also say: "You do not need to worry about death. When it comes, there is nothing you can do about it. So, are you enjoying your life?"

And that will be all of my dharma talk. Thank you.

"Why buy a cookbook when you are hungry? Just eat!"

> *[W]hen we sit in meditation we do not sit in time. Time causes suffering. When we walk, we are not going anywhere. Space also causes suffering. We arrive in an eternal moment or beyond. Just in arriving here. No word will explain what this is here.*

There was a story that was written in a book that said: "Is that so?" Some may have read that story. Another story was about an empty teacup. And there was another one about a sifter that was thrown into some water—throw your whole self in.

The stories that are told in Buddhism do not really tell you about the experience, but they tell you about moving towards something, or that you are already standing in it—you just never drink. That your suffering, or thirst that is looking for something, is basically delusion—it is not there.

So, we look for things in time or a future—preparing ourselves to receive something that is never here. Thus we continue to thirst. Instead of letting ourselves go into the story. Into the here and now. From empty teacups, to "is that so", to the sifter that is in the water. It can only be done now. Nowhere else. So, if you are planning to do zazen tomorrow or after you leave here—it cannot be done. Impossible.

If the dharma is true, then things are constantly changing. So, the being that is making that decision in the here and now will never be there in the future. Yes, there will be someone else—a different breath.

So, when we sit in meditation we do not sit in time. Time causes suffering. When we walk, we are not going anywhere. Space also causes suffering. We arrive in an eternal moment or beyond. Just in arriving here. No word will explain what this is here. Koans point to it. Stories point to it. But the experience is not in the story itself. It is only a form. Most koans are just forms that are empty. Void of a thought or memory of it. In other words, it can only be tasted right now that you are here.

So, how many of us are waiting to drink this water somewhere in the future? Preparing for this drink?

So, here I am at the Cleveland Buddhist Temple—sitting, walking, chanting. I hear the boiler downstairs grumbling. It seems as if it assists me in my sitting to not attach to it. It is on its karmic path so I do not need to worry about it. "Back to the breath," it tells me. Just like the clappers. So, a lot of things like cars and trains I attach to—but they are on their karmic path. That experience sets me free to experience this path right here. Almost as if it corrects me and says: "I am doing my thing, why aren't you doing yours?"

So, here I am with yet another story. Still using words. But pointing to something that has no words, explanation, or anything else. One might say: "When will we drink from the water and stop this preparing?"

Reverend Ogui once talked about how most of us are hungry for something yet instead of eating we go and buy a cookbook. We will sit here and nod in agreement, then we will go and buy a book. Then we will engage in words and conversation in a coffee shop—instead of eating.

We cannot wake up ourselves. Others are necessary. The mind cannot see itself, so it cannot really change itself—it only reacts. So, in Jodo Shin Shoo they talk about others from the other side—such as the boiler. Just stories—they use stories such as "Hell". We will send them down some silk to release someone from hell—but he does not bring others so we cut the silk before he gets up. We tell all kind of stories about how we are interdependent. And we hear these stories but we do not let them go. They are very great stories. We like them, so we hold on to them. Right? They have stories for that story. Right? We like these stories so we hold on to them.

So, they have another story that says: If you see the Buddha on the road, kill him. Let it go. Reverend Ogui often talked about walking in the forest but never stopping—just going right through. Other stories. All kinds of stories. Stories about rivers converging into the ocean. When you are in the river, you are going along with the current and you want to get off and go to the shore because you see something. But you have never seen the awe of the vast ocean of wisdom. So, he says keep going. But I am always attracted by something. So I am going to get out of that water and check something out. But these are all stories that do not really say what they say. Stories about looking for something such as the ox pictures that are downstairs. Talking about something hard like ice and something soft like water. Seeming like they are separate, but they are the same thing.

So, here I am at the Cleveland Buddhist Temple. Zazen is the name of something. Kenhin is the name of something. The chants that I practice. They all may seem as if they are not my life—I only practice them sometimes. But yet and still they are just stories to go through, through, and through. When you are tired of stories—drink.

So, how many ways can you change words around? When you get tired of playing with them—comparing this one and that one—when you get tired of them, drink...take a breath...go beyond.

And that will be all of my dharma talk. Thank you.

"[A]ll thought is a 'future event.'"

> *Do not wish for things to be other than they are . . . . These conditions arise out of limitless wisdom and boundless compassion.*

About 5 o'clock every morning, I am up. Sometimes 4:30. I prepare to go outside—me and Buster (that's the dog). [Laughter.] And, I look at Buster and say: "It is cold outside." He just wags his tail and jumps around. It seems that he is already prepared to go outside. So, I will ask Buster: "Do you wish that it would be a little warmer?"

My teacher once said: "When sitting, do not wish for anything different but what is there." Years ago we used to sit in this Temple when it was cold—before they got the new boiler downstairs and there was only a linoleum floor with concrete under it. People would be dressed similar to you with your wool hat and scarf on. And we would come here and the floor would be cold and we would sit. We would even do sesshins—and walk and chant. We also sat when it was truly hot outside. We would sit and sweat. These are the conditions of infinite wisdom and boundless compassion. So, why not enjoy yourself—since things are so impermanent.

One time I was over a lady's house who used to sit here—she is in Canada now, in the French part of Canada. She speaks French and has a practice up there. Her name was Bobbi Popovich. Her Buddhist name was Snow Tiger. And, we were all over there and the mosquitoes were biting me. And I complained about how they were eating me up. And my teacher said: "They have very short lives. Let them eat." [Laughter.] I was wishing for them not to be around, but he reminded me that they have very short lives—so, I should let them eat.

So, here I am in certain conditions. And, yet and still I suffer. Instead of arriving in these conditions and becoming a part of them—I suffer. Always not seeing the conditions, but rather seeing my thirst. How I wish it would be. Looking at the flowers and the candle—moving on. Still, I want things to be how I want them to be. I thirst for a little more warmth and for the spring to come.

I asked the people yesterday: "What would you like to do with your life?" They were all here for something. All of them wished to be somewhere else or something different. Every action was in preparation for a future event. Yes. So, here I am in a future event. You may not believe this. You might say: "I am here." But basically, all thought is a "future event." All you have to do is look at it. It will go back into the past. See its mistakes and accomplishments. And then project into the future. Yes, all you have to do is look at it. It moves back and then says: "Now I can prepare for something."

So, I know that when it gets cold outside, I can prepare. I look back to this same time last year. And we believe that this is very useful. But we always escape the present moment—right now. I might ask: "When will I depend on the wisdom of Amidha Buddha—infinite wisdom and boundless compassion?" When will I come to this "Enlightenment"—to the realization that I and it, this present moment, are one? When will I come that? When will I arrive in this present moment—in sitting, walking, chanting . . . in life itself?

A couple of days ago, Joe and I were driving around and I was aware of the snowflakes dancing around. He was talking about his immediate problem. Of course, it was something that happened in a past because a "problem" cannot exist right now. So, something happened in the past that causes him suffering in the here and now. So, he cannot experience the here and now.

I was looking at the snowflakes. They were moving around while we were driving. And it was amazing that each one was doing something different. Not one of them was going the same direction or doing anything else the same. I looked at Joe and said: "Life itself is like this. Not one of them is the same or doing the same thing or going to the same place. They are all on their karmic path. You should trust that the snowflake does what it does."

Some would say that is a poor analogy to human life. But other parts of the dharma—snowflakes, trees and the wind—are all interconnected. When the wind blows hard a person—just like the snowflake—moves a little differently. [Laughter.] And we watch these truths—the chills and the flinches that happen. Everything is moving just a little bit differently because one of the things they are connected to—the wind—is moving differently.

So, here we are, in the dharma. But this life of mine is not interesting to me because I am not like the snowflake. I have dulled my senses via the delusion that I am a "human being" instead of the dharma or naturalness itself. A "human being" has what they call morals, ethics, and a value system. So, the human being is an actor. So, we act because of training. And we act because of past reference. So we do certain things because we are human beings—rather than being like the snowflake, or the dharma, or naturalness.

So, Joe asked me what he should do about his problem. I said: "The problem is not really there." So he asked whether he should meditate. I said: "That is not really natural. I do not know any animal that sits like we sit." [Laughter.] I told him that I think the only reason that formal meditation was created was because of extremes. So, we go from our hectic, thirst-driven extreme to an extreme form of stillness. But what is in between these two extremes? Will they bring us to naturalness? Will one, perhaps via riddles, wake us up so we can move just a little bit like the snowflake, just a little bit like the trees, just a little bit in nature—being aware of This. Not aware of it intellectually, but aware of it like a fish surrounded by water does not know it is wet. Will that awareness ever drift in? When it does, we will surely say: "Wow!"

Wake up to This. It is amazing, the interdependence of all things. That awareness, not the one the mind can point to or grab. There are no words there. It is like drinking water. A child may come upon a glass of water. One adult may explain to the child that this is "water" or "H2O." The glass is solid, the water is clear, cold, refreshing, and wet. Another person may just come up, take the glass, drink the water and say: "Ah!" [Laughter.] Yes. There is no "water." There is just life itself—interdependent. No words to explain it. Gate gate para sam gate. Gone. Far gone. Beyond "water"—no such thing, just: "Ah!"—life itself. The fish does not swim around saying: "Water."

So, here I am. Sitting in these extremes and doing these extreme things. Never saying: "Ah!" Always suffering for something different. Every move I make is for the future and for something different. When will I wake up right here?

How many of you know about koans? How do you know about koans? Did your teacher give you one?

[Student: Through reading.]

Did you read the answers of the koans? Most books have answers to the koans. The intellectual answer to the koan is like explaining the glass of water to the child in words. But the intent of the koan is to produce the "Ah!" of awareness when the words of the mind tie themselves up and there are no words to explain but yet and still life itself opens up. In this awareness there may not be any thirst or suffering. Time may disappear. Yes. And, the thing called space or perception might even disappear. So, we will arrive here. No where else.

People came to the Temple yesterday and I asked about the alter—the flowers and the candle. We had already talked about the oranges and the apples. Are they trying to become "better" or seeking to be something other than they are?

And I told them about the Buddha that sat right here, and Annanda and Mahakashapa. And I told them about the twirling of the flower. You have heard of that? When the Buddha twirled the flower, what happened to Mahakashapa?

[Student: He awakened.]

Awakened! When he twirled the flower. George, right?

[Student: Yes.]

So, if I was to twirl the flower and enlightenment struck—would "George" see it?

[Student: Maybe not.]

There would be no "George."

And so the Buddha realized this and said: "Wow!" And the dharma was transmitted. Naturalness and the words "fully awake." Beyond "water" and the intellectual mind.

So, when George speaks of Mahakashapa he believes there was one and it awakened. No. And, yes.

I think that will be all of my dharma talk. Thank you.

"Drop it!"

> *Return to counting your breath and wake up. . . .*
> *[S]taying there with the breath—the gong rings. . . . [T]he*
> *breath is interdependent with everything. As the wind*
> *blows, one blade of grass falls and everything that is*
> *around—every person, every man, every star . . .*
> *everything, is changed.*

Conditions change, do they not? Not too long ago we had a sesshin here. It was the Saturday that just passed. It was very cold. [*Laughter.*] But today it is hot. Conditions change. They are constantly changing.

My teacher once said: "Do not wish for either hot or cold. Just sit in it."

Which one is preferred: the heat or the cold? When it is too cold, we wish it to be hot. When it is too hot, we wish it to be cold. So, when will we be satisfied? Or, when will it be enough just the way it is.

Conditions are constantly changing. So, sitting in the cold or sitting in the heat, trying to wait for it to cool down or heat up, in time it seems like it will never happen. Return to counting the breath. One may say: "The gong has struck." Yes. And in the end they will say: "That wasn't too bad." But sitting in it, thinking about *it*, it is horrible. Return to counting the breath, arriving in each one right here.

Here we are at the Cleveland Buddhist Temple. Conditions are changing. Earlier today it was raining. I once heard Reverend Ogui say: "Sit like a mountain. Rain may fall. Snow may come. The wind may blow. But a mountain just sits. Empty yourself of everything and become a true mountain."

Empty yourself of what? Your opinions about the rain. Empty yourself of everything and become a true mountain. "It is too wet. It is too cold. It is too windy." Once we draw to these words, it seems as if they bring suffering. But these words are a form. And Reverend Ogui would hit the clappers and say: "Drop it. Drop it."

All your opinions about words such as "ordinary mind is the way" are just that—opinions. We try to figure the words out. We use intellect to figure them out. Drop it!

He would use a koan: "Things are not what they seem to be, nor are they otherwise." So, a person would sit and be thinking about what they are going to say when Reverend Ogui asks them what the koan means. And they would be sitting and thinking about the koan instead of returning to the breath. Thinking about the koan, bringing about suffering.

The form brings us to the breath because it cannot figure out the answer. So, let them go. Return to counting your breath and wake up. Here I am and words are arising in my head. Maybe all kinds of different things are arising. It seems like every time I go back to the breath, only a minute or two has gone by. Then I go back to thinking. And another minute goes by. This is taking all day, isn't it? [*Laughter.*] But staying there with the breath—the gong rings. And whatever it is, it is not in words that we answer.

There is a practice where you are given a koan by a sensei and the sensei will ask you about the koan and you will answer with words and the sensei will tell you to go sit a little longer. Words are not it. The intellectual mind is not it. So, here we sit using words such as "nirvana," "sukhavati," "enlightenment," "ordinary mind"—all kinds of words. But in "The Last Samurai" they had "no mind." So, what word is there for "no mind"? What word? One moves toward the breath, then one comes up and says: "I must have the answer." It is almost like a preconceived idea that I will get the answer here and then I will tell it in the future. Does that do anyone any good? Or, when the question is asked, is the answer not already known? But one has to let go of preconceived ideas and answer straight and direct. Not from what was read in the past or from preconceived ideas, but from right here. As soon as the koan is said, there is the answer. It and the answer arrive at the same time. Yes. So, one will be saying: "I am 'in tune' with this life—life itself—as it arises."

There is another tape I listen to that asks why we do not embrace the now right here. And this tape says the reason is that this moment is too powerful. Yes. So, we create futures and pasts. Something that we can control and design. But the now is too powerful. And someone might say: "What do you mean, it is too powerful? It is only one breath?" But the breath is interdependent with everything. As the wind blows, one blade of grass falls and everything that is around—every person, every man, every star . . . everything, is changed. A moment like that is just too powerful for our mind to grasp. So, we create a future, a problem. We speak our ignorance.

Sit right here. When you are moving towards words like "zazen" and then "kenhin" and then "chanting" you are creating a future. You are not right here. You are not beyond the words. They are not both arising at the same time. Yes.

So, Reverand Ogui would go around with his koans and he would ask you these questions. And you would say your answers. And he would grunt and walk on. Next time you may use the same answer or a different one. And still you would get the grunt. And it always seemed like the answers had been preconstructed during the sitting. A person could be giving a talk right in front of you, and you would be trying to figure out the answer. You would be sitting and breathing, and still trying to figure out the answer. When there is no question and no answer—there is only this right here.

So, does anyone know anything about that? Has anyone read anything about that? When there is no question, there is no answer. Yes. Mahasyakapa and the twirling of the flower. No self. No question. No answer. No "awake." Just in the here and now: "Thank you." Not thinking about the question. Not thinking about an answer.

So, here we are. Still beginners in meditation. Sitting, walking, chanting. But here we are. Reverend Ogui would say: "Since you are here, why not?" Why not? You can always go outside. But since you are here, why not?

And that will be all of my dharma talk. Thank you.

"Holiday"

> *When the conditions are right, the snow will fall. No one can stop it. The only reason I do not see that is because I am always outside the conditions. I am always trying to make something happen. Instead of realizing there is no making.... It just happens—there it is.*

So, here we are. Sitting at the Cleveland Buddhist Temple on the day after a holiday called Christmas. This word: "holiday"—I have been trying to figure out whether it really exists. [*Laughter.*] We are so prone, or habituated, to believe that it really exists. So expectation, time, and different things of suffering go beyond its true meaning and obstruct us. So, I ask: What did you get for the holiday? Did you receive the gift that stops the thirst?

In the Four Noble Truths it talks about the thirst. The thirst of ignorance. Did you get the gift that stops this thirst? Did you receive that? Yes? Then one may say: It is not about what have I have received—but what I have ceased looking for. Because I have received the truth that my life is right here.

When I slow down or stop, it seems like the world is moving fast and going somewhere. The Tao Te Ching talks about the baby, or the being, that seems like it has no place to go. Everybody else is busy, everybody else has a purpose. But I am dull and so forth, with no place to go. I am wandering with no directions. But yet and still I am nurtured by the Great Mother. And it seems as if everyone is in this thing and going somewhere. Yet and still sometimes I sit and it moves slowly. "Holiday." The word disappears.

It seems as if there is something that is forgotten. If you ever go out when there is a holiday you'll find a huge market of people around. And what was forgotten is beyond the Oneness from which all of this came together. The interdependent Other. The constant changing of it. Varied. Transitory. Constantly moving. This huge mass. Beyond One. Sit long enough and the rumble and the noise is there, but just look and go beyond. No noise. This great mass.

Everything is moving towards it—that Oneness and beyond, toward what cannot be explained.

So, "Holidays." What did they bring to you? What did you receive?

Holidays and other things bring about what they call "family." They come in from different places and it has something that says we should use our morals and ethics during these times in deciding how to act and respond to one another. We should use kindness and let bygones be bygones. Now, let's be civil for a change. Let's just stop moving from our busy lives and work, and sit down and be civil. Yes. So, it brings about that idea. But after the holidays, who cares anymore? [*Laughter.*] That idea winds up and we go back to the hustle and bustle.

So, this word called "holiday"—let's just throw it away. This word called "civil"—let's get rid of it. Let's go through the words to infinite wisdom and boundless compassion. The words suggest I am permanent. Instead of observing a day such as a holiday, since things are impermanent, shouldn't we observe every moment—constantly changing in that mass? Yes.

So, who will get rid of it, this word "holiday," and move toward interdependence and impermanence? The Way is to observe our lives as they are in the here and now, beyond the labels. Then our lives would be amazing. Beyond kindness and beyond morals and ethics and trying to be something.

When the conditions are right, the snow will fall. No one can stop it. The only reason I do not see that is because I am always outside the conditions. I am always trying to make something happen. Instead of realizing there is no making. The laws of causality tell us there is no making. It just happens—there it is. Karma is put into it with action. Karma is neither good nor bad. It is just karma. Just action. But yet and still the five skandhas or aggregates of man try to describe it *after* it has happened. So, we say that was good or that was bad. Oh, I should have been a better person. I shouldn't have said that. But not till *after* it has happened. When will one wake up and realize this? Move toward something like: "It is too soon to tell." Studying one's life. Arriving into impermanence—these conditions. Yes. Instead of so much arriving into delusion, the skandhas, the aggregates, the forms. Tied up by semantics. No. Just go beyond.

So, if we were to take the word "holiday" and throw it out there we would have semantics—everyone would have their own version of it. But we are all arriving into the same thing. Pointing toward something. Go beyond this. Till that word disappears and this, right here, the breath, everything beyond holiday.

I had Buster, my dog, outside earlier today on Christmas. And Buster, for some reason, didn't know that he shouldn't be expecting his usual walk. He saw me preparing the ham and doing different things, but he had a routine and there's no holiday from that routine. Life to its fullest—its true nature. His true nature is not that different from mine. I watch him. He uses the bathroom, he eats, he plays. He doesn't build houses or anything like that. He doesn't work, so he plays. He has feelings. Has some kind of consciousness because he knows where to sniff and where he's been. We walk down the street and he sees the crossing stripes and he knows that's where we go to the other side. So, he is kind of true to his nature. Me? No. It's a "holiday." Why am I up so early? I don't have time to be walking in the park and playing with you. I have things to do. But Buster has his routine.

So, are holidays our true nature or are they days that take us out of our true nature such that we become actors playing the part of "good people"? Yes. Bearing gifts. We can even call it false gifts.

So, here we are. Sitting at the Cleveland Buddhist Temple on the day after a holiday called Christmas. One would say: "My life is interesting." Some people have the belief that it is over. Don't have to worry about it again till next year. All I have to do is make it through the first of the year. That's the last one. Then life will go back to the norm. We will see this as hectic, but we won't really learn from the dharma or past experience. So, where are the struggles and what makes them so exciting? Others wait for them.

Something's going to happen on this day. What makes them so exciting? Is it a delusion or a false belief? For Buster every day is exciting. As soon as he gets ready to go outside he is bouncing up and down. Every day is exciting. He doesn't know he should be jumping at least another 5 or 6 feet on Christmas because something is going to happen. [*Laughter.*]

And that will be all of my dharma talk. Thank you.

"Have a cup of tea."

> *There is constant change. That is my life. So, wherever I am in this moment—shouldn't I pay attention to it? This moment is never to repeat itself. Shouldn't I participate? Sit down, and have a cup of tea. Where is the rush to go somewhere?*

I have arrived here. Looking at the flowers as they are wilting or moving on. I use so much effort to do something when there is nothing to do here. Walking in and having a seat. Zen meditation and walking meditation, one can say, brings us to another realization: that our life is right here.

I listen to people like me that talk a lot. Explaining things. Having conversations. Discussing morals. Exchanging for interaction. Because I believe there is such a thing as others and if I don't do this my life is boring. Yes, my life is boring. So, let's talk about some Buddhism. Let's talk about some Taoism. Let's talk about these things. Let's excite the ego or the delusion of self. Even though I am right here and there is nothing to talk about. Because, things are constantly changing.

Yesterday, some young people were here sitting in meditation. And I told them about wanting to go somewhere very, very fast. Wanting to grow up very, very fast. Get a career, get somewhere. Dharma is already saying that this is what is going to happen. I'm going to grow. Just like all other things. So, why are you in a hurry to get there? Sit down. Relax. Enjoy yourself. One would say to them: "Have a cup of tea." A cookie to go with it, or a piece of cake. Don't overindulge. And make the tea a ceremony. Take a little time there. Arriving in the here and now, not off in some future. Here, where the conditions are also noted, not secondary.

How do forms pass? One's whole self takes me through. Takes me through the form. When the form disappears one could say: "This." Going through the forms and arriving into This. I was talking with someone about Taoist philosophy and how they're always talking about "This". What is "This"?

I also ask people, what do they see that is different about the altar? One woman came in and sat in meditation and I asked her what did she see that had changed during her meditation. Some of them had changed their position. So, they could see things they had not seen before—like the candle that had been hidden from view. But no one said "This" is changing. The candle has gotten smaller. The flowers have died a little more. One person said when they came here there was one thing there. When they sat back down there was another thing. There is constant change. That is my life. So, wherever I am in this moment—shouldn't I pay attention to it? This moment is never to repeat itself. Shouldn't I participate? Sit down, and have a cup of tea. Where is the rush to go somewhere?

My teacher always asked: "Why did you come here? Who brought you?" And there would be various answers and he would say none of these are wrong or right—just answer. Then he would come back the next day or the next week and he would say, "Who brought you here?" The answers and the person would have changed. And the answers sometimes will be different. The answers will have changed. And my teacher would smile a little bit. And then the next time: "Who brought you here?" And there would be something different. Other people might say something. Someone else may say what you wanted to say and all of a sudden the answer may have changed again. Conditions are different. But when I have moved beyond Oneness, my answer is always the same.

So, does the dog have Buddha nature? What do you say? If you become a part of the conditions, instead of outside the conditions, how could the answer be different? Breath. Another breath. Only one breath. Only one condition. Not compared with past. Beyond that. Beyond linear time. Arriving into "This."

We chant in the Heart Sutra we say "no eyes," "no mind," "no...no...no." All the way down. "Form is sunyata, sunyata is form." "Gone, gone, way gone to the other shore. All the way gone to the other shore." It talks about that. After I reach this shore, there's no answer. So, it's constantly changing. Conditions, causes, all point to suffering.

That will be all of my dharma talk. Thank you.

APPENDIX I
The Bodhisattva's Vow

When I (a student of the Dharma) look at the real form of the universe, all is the never-failing manifestation of the mysterious truth of Tathagata. In any event, in any moment, and in any place, none can be other than the marvellous revelation of its glorious light.

This realization made our founding teachers and virtuous Zen leaders extend tender care, with the heart of worshipping, to animals and birds, and indeed to all beings. This realization teaches us that our daily food, drink, clothes, and protections of life are the warm flesh and blood, the merciful incarnation of Buddha Who can be ungrateful or not respectful to each and every thing, as well as to human beings!

Even though someone may be a fool, be warm and compassionate. If by any chance such a person should turn against us, become a sworn enemy and abuse and persecute us, we should sincerely bow down with humble language, in reverent belief that he or she is the merciful avatar of Buddha, who uses devices to emancipate us from sinful karma that has been produced and accumulated upon ourselves by our own egoistic delusion and attachment through countless cycles of kalpas.

Then on each moment's flash of our thought there will grow a lotus flower, and on each lotus flower will be revealed a Buddha. These Buddhas will glorify Sukhavati, the Pure Land, every moment and everywhere.

May we extend this mind over all beings so that we and the world together may attain maturity in Buddha's wisdom.

APPENDIX II
The Heart Sutra

Avalokitesvara, the Bodhisattva of compassion, doing deep Prajna Paramita, clearly saw that the five skandhas are Sunyata, thus transcending misfortune and suffering.

O Shariputra, form is no other than Sunyata, Sunyata is no other than form. Form is exactly Sunyata, Sunyata exactly form. Feeling, thought, volition, and consciousness are likewise like this.

O Shariputra, remember, dharma is fundamentally Sunyata. No birth, no death. Nothing is defiled, nothing is pure. Nothing can increase, nothing can decrease. Hence: no eyes, no ears, no nose, no tongue, no body, no mind: no seeing, no hearing, no smelling, no tasting, no touching, no thinking: no world of sight, no world of consciousness. No ignorance and no end to ignorance. No old age and death and no end to old age and death. No suffering, no craving, no extinction, no path: no wisdom, no attainment.

Indeed, there is nothing to be attained; the Bodhisattva relies on Prajna Paramita with no hindrance in the mind – no hindrance, therefore no fear. Far beyond upside down views, at last Nirvana. Past, present, and future, all Buddhas, Bodhisattvas, rely on Prajna Paramita and therefore reach the most supreme enlightenment.

Therefore know: Prajna Paramita is the greatest dharani, the brightest dharani, the highest dharani, the incomparable dharani. It completely clears all suffering. This is the truth, not a lie. So set forth the Prajna Paramita dharani, set forth this dharani and say:

Gate, Gate, Paragate, Parasamgate, Bodhi Svaha.